The Worry-Free Wealth Guide to Stock Market Investing

How to Prosper in the Wall Street Jungle

READ THIS OR GO BROKE!

Scott "Doc" Brown, Ph.D.
"The Wallet Doctor"

Discover how an 18-Year-Old McDonald's minimum wage cook becomes a millionaire in 50 years. Enroll in this essential community on stock investing now at http://worryfreewealth.com/offers/.

For general information on our other products and services or for technical support, please contact our **Customer Care Department** at support@worryfreewealth.com.

Photography by Miguel Rios Bracero: http://bit.ly/2qMz5Nl

Publisher's Cataloging-In-Publication Data
(Prepared by The Donohue Group, Inc.)

Names: Brown, Scott (Scott Matthew), Ph.D.
Title: The Worry-Free Wealth guide to stock market investing: how to prosper in the Wall Street jungle / Scott "Doc" Brown, Ph.D., "The Wallet Doctor."
Description: 2nd Edition. | Las Vegas, NV: Worry-Free Wealth, [2017] | "Includes 7 hours of free audios."—Cover. | Includes bibliographical references and index.
Identifiers: ISBN 978-0-9788345-1-7 | ISBN 0-9788345-1-8 | ISBN 978-0-9788345-2-4 (ebook) | ISBN 0-9788345-2-6 (ebook)
Subjects: LCSH: Stocks—United States. | Investments—United States. | Mutual funds—United States. | Financial literacy—United States.
Classification: LCC HG4661 .B76 2017 (print) | LCC HG4661 (ebook) | DDC 332.63/22—dc23

Kindle & Interior design and preparation by Soumi Goswami.

Website: https://www.linkedin.com/in/soumigoswami

Contact Soumi directly at soumi.goswami.pub@gmail.com

Table of Contents

Introduction

Wall Street is only seven blocks long, but is possibly the most important street on Earth. It has fueled some of the greatest economic expansions ever known; it has plunged millions into poverty and ruin. It is home to the oldest, largest and most respected stock exchange in America, the New York Stock Exchange. It is also home of some of the largest financial institutions led by the most cunning and ruthless money mongers in the world. This reading is designed to educate you to give you a good shot at surviving the complex and confusing maze that Wall Street uses to extract a profit from the unsuspecting public.

Generations before us have fallen prey to the financial predators of Wall Street. I just finished watching the movie *Cinderella Man* where Russell Crowe portrays the true story of world champion boxer Jim Braddock. What I found fascinating was that both Braddock and his manager, Gould (not to be confused with Jay Gould, the notorious manipulator), invested all their money in the stock market at the end of the 1920s just before the crash that

Throughout the book, you will see little icons such as:

Tips to help you make money.

Traps that Wall Street uses to ensnare you.

Facts that are fun to know!

precipitated the Great Depression. They, like many people who were attracted to the stock market at the wrong time, ended up bankrupt. Braddock lost all of his money, a substantial sum, as a champion boxer in the Roaring Twenties, and ended up broke, living in bread lines and on the dole.

Both these men knew that the promoters behind the fights made all of the money in the boxing industry with the least risk financially and physically. Like most Americans, they lost in the stock market because they lacked the inside connections to the forces behind the scenes, or simply lacked the experience to know when to buy low and when to sell high with the insiders and manipulators.[1] Neither of them stopped to think that perhaps there exists an industry of promotion driving the stock market that is not only based on hype, but also serves the agenda of powerful individuals in corporate America, the federal government and the equity capital industry also known as the stock market.

These two men who knew so much about boxing knew *nothing* about the stock market. Ironically, while these men suffered financially, a few individuals who were either experienced investors or "inside" and hence, "in the know", sold out at the top after having bought low years earlier – they lived lives of luxury during the Depression. You don't hear much about these successful investors, because they didn't say much, and they certainly did not care to teach the public what they knew.

---

[1] An insider is a shareholder who owns more than 5% of a publicly traded corporation, or an officer or director of the company. I further class them as visible insiders if they must report their trading to the SEC and invisible insiders who are manipulators that buy individually under the reporting requirements of the SEC yet control a large enough percentage of the float as a group to manipulate the price of the stock over a period of years. Dark pools are an example

Times are no different today than when Braddock was struggling to raise a family. We have just witnessed an equities industry caught in scandals of inside trading, false corporate accounting records, and inside executives dumping their option-vested stock on an unsuspected public as an insider-controlled network of stock brokerages, brokers, mutual funds and the media hyped up the "bull market of the century." These are just a few of the savage beasts in the stock market jungle that will eat you alive financially if you don't educate yourself and become savvy.

Before you read on, make sure you enroll in my free basic stock investment training to get access to 7 hours (and more) of free audio and video as promised on the cover of this book. This will add another dimension to your kindle reading,

Discover how an 18-Year-Old McDonald's minimum wage cook becomes a millionaire in 50 years. Enroll in this essential community on stock investing now.

Link: http://worryfreewealth.com/offers/

You will notice that this document is sparse on graphics. That is done to keep the download speed high on kindle. I give you rich visual detail in the free course above. **-Doc Brown a.k.a. The Wallet Doctor**

P.S. Make sure to join this community's Facebook group here.

Link: https://www.facebook.com/groups/FinancialAnswers/

Chapter 1: A Brief History of Stock Investing

Francis was born and raised in a family of Swedish immigrants in a small town near Atlantic, Iowa. As a youth, she had the striking good looks of a beauty queen, but found herself married to a jealous and violent alcoholic. She endured a painful marriage but, after her first husband died, she met and fell in love with Leonard, a gentle wealthy dentist, who personally attended to William Randolph Hearst's family. She was 75 when she very happily remarried. Tragically, Leonard died a short time later and Francis received an inheritance of $85,000 in an account with a nationwide brokerage. The full-service broker who managed her account was named Joe. He was known for pushing overpriced stocks on the elderly. Full-service brokers have been caught doing this.

Francis grew concerned when she stopped getting her Pacific Power and Light dividends. When she called Joe, he reminded her that she had instructed him to sell it and buy Pacific Lighting. She replied, *"You told me that you thought it was a good stock. I said I might buy it—not that I would buy it!"* She didn't realize

Trap: The history of investing teaches us that a few people in-the-know on the "inside" track do everything they can to buy shares of a company low when the public isn't paying attention and then sell it back high after exciting optimistic rumors about the firm have been leaked to the press!

that her casual conversation with a financial counselor she trusted—her full-service broker—had given Joe the authorization to sell her good stock and buy bad stock. She called him because she didn't know that he had moved her out of Pacific Power and Light and into Pacific Lighting without her desire. She found out with an empty feeling in the pit of her stomach that he had allowed the stock to drop to nothing without calling her even though he had been aware of the problem the whole time. She took his word and lost it all. A kind, serene and gentle old woman, she tried to complain, but Joe easily held her back. Her son, Delano Max Brown, died of cancer less than a year after Leonard. When Del's wife Barbara became aware of the problem, she had no idea what Francis' rights were, so the $85,000 just disappeared under the guidance of a full service, Wall Street-endorsed thief. It was finally getting around the valley that Joe was recommending bad stock to other retirees, but since he was selective and targeted the elderly who did not know their rights, he was never prosecuted.

If I had known what I know today, things would be quite different—the Federal authorities don't take too kindly to full-service brokers who swindle the elderly. The nationwide brokerage Dean, Whitter, Reynolds would have been forced to fully repay the little old woman all the money (and then some) that their licensed broker had swindled. This is because Francis was my grandmother, and a good part of the motivation that led me to master my understanding of money and earn a Ph.D. in finance.

One promise I make you is that, as my student, I will teach you how to invest in the stock market in such a way that the full-service thieves of Wall Street can never damage your account! Wall Street, however, is also a place that can make you rich.

Here's its history.

Centuries ago, investing was utter chaos. The roots of investment trace back thousands of years to ancient **Greece**. Ship captains offered a share of their profits to those in society who were able and willing to share in the risk of financing a trading voyage to faraway lands across the sea. Investing was an "all or nothing" gamble of personal savings. The ship might return with riches (hence the saying "my ship came in") or might be lost at sea and not return at all.

The **Romans** sold stock as well in huge civic construction projects that were beyond the means of a single businessman. Stockholders made handsome profits by investing in companies that built roads and aqueducts for the Roman government. Investment was restricted to Roman citizens. The slaves that built the projects did not benefit.

It wasn't until the 1600s that investing took a giant leap forward when the first shares of stock in a corporation were created in the **Dutch East Indies Company** in Holland. Like the Greek seafaring merchants before them, the Dutch needed capital for international trade. This investment, however, was different because people bought a stake in the trading company—not in a single ocean voyage or civic project. **Speculation** followed because investors could sell their shares to one another over time without waiting for the ships to come in.

The stock price could rise or fall on the faintest of rumors, spreading panic in the world's first stock exchange. Rising markets created new riches and market crashes wiped investors out. Those who lost money were of the wealthy class of nobles and merchants. They blamed their losses on pushy stock brokers. When the inevitable crash came, the citizens of modest means were not affected because they had not been able to invest. The general attitude of the common citizen was that the upper class wealthy gamblers had gotten what they deserved—the eventual collapse of the Dutch East Indies Company did not cause panic among the public.

Investors' opinions of stock brokers sunk even lower in the 1700s. In Paris, an escaped murderer sold stock. There were also other spectacular instances of fraud in the French stock market. **John Law,** one of the first "executive insiders", working secretly with stock brokers, swindled the public with worthless shares of stock in his **Company of the West** that he fictitiously claimed owned gold mines in the then French-owned Louisiana Territory. He guaranteed a 40% return and created one of the first recorded public con jobs eventually known as a **Ponzi scheme.** The stock was bid up in a buying frenzy and then crashed, wiping out people who bought too late as the "house of paper" collapsed.

In London, stock brokers lured investors into a Ponzi scheme with stories of a secret device that turned chicken into sheep. Sheep at the time were worth more than chickens and the value of these stocks skyrocketed until people came to their senses and stopped bidding prices up. The **inside manipulators** started to sell out at astronomical levels and the price dropped a little. Experienced investors not on the inside track of the manipulation started to worry as they saw the price weaken. Soon everyone realized the rise was over but it was too late. Panic set in, and collapse followed. This is how a market crash occurred then, and still occurs today in a frenzy.

Welcome to this training! Left to Right: CEO Dave Watkins, Doc Brown (Me), Annie Mustafa, MBA, Daniel Hall, J.D., Hon. Antonio Colorado, J.D., Mark Schwartz, M.D.

WALL STREET

Despite unscrupulous brokers and numerous Ponzi schemes, stocks helped make Europe the colonial and economic power-house of the world. Stocks would do the same for the United States of America beginning on a short muddy footpath named Wall Street. **Wall Street** was so named when New York was a tiny colonial outpost. Pilgrims in 1653 built a wall to keep out Indians. About 100 years later, the wall was gone but the path that ran alongside it had become the center of New York City's commerce and society. The heart of the young city already had a dark side. On Wall Street was the auction block to sell slaves and the pillory for public humiliation.[2] **George**

---

[2] A pillory is a wooden framework erected on a post, with holes for securing the head and hands, formerly used to expose the offender to public derision.

Washington was sworn in as the first U.S. president on Wall Street in 1789.

Wall Street was where merchants met underneath a buttonwood tree to auction off stocks, mainly in banks and mines, while collecting a commission on every sale. This informal open air stock market lasted until 1792, when 24 merchants signed a document called the "**Buttonwood Agreement**." The pact was intended to avoid government regulation of street auctions and it blocked newcomers from entering the stock brokering business.

This formed the **New York Stock Exchange Board,** where brokers met inside the **Tontine Coffee House** for two informal stock auctions per day—the public was not allowed to participate. If you wanted to trade in stock, you had to hire a broker to do it. This made stock market data opaque and caused the public to be less informed about what was going on inside. In the original open auction system, where everybody could hear everything, people knew a lot more. As is the case today, what is good for Wall Street is frequently not good for you.

Fact: In 1789, the first U.S. government bonds were traded under the buttonwood tree in the open-air stock market on Wall Street – $80 million worth to pay for the then recent war against England!

The new coffee house auctions were indoor sessions where auctioneers sold stocks one by one, allowing brokers to regulate themselves to prevent more flagrant forms of fraud and abuse that occurred regularly on the street outside. Only stocks of real companies were traded, and the sales were recorded. These procedures created a false air of respectability. Stock brokering became perceived as a reputable profession.

During the auctions, prices for shares of stock were quoted in increments of an eighth of a dollar or just **eighths**. This practice can be traced back to a time when people carried Spanish milled dollars and cut them into pieces of eight for change. In the beginning, only 30 companies were traded inside the exchange—banks, cargo insurance companies and construction firms that built bridges and piers—yet only a handful of fearless investors dared buy them. The general public was afraid of the stock market because, unlike bonds, if the company went bankrupt the stockholders lost everything. Stocks were for two types of people; outright speculators or people trying to take control of the company.

The struggle for respectability on Wall Street brought only a short period of limited success to the brokers and auctioneers that controlled it. With time, the less reputable trading of stocks resumed out front on the street among the brokers who weren't allowed to join the exchange board. Disputes between these **curb trading** stock brokers were settled with fists.

In 1832, an invention allowed news to flash across the United States called the **telegraph**. In the world of finance, information is power. The telegraph was a godsend. The inventor, **Samuel Morse**, opened a demonstration office near the stock exchange charging 25¢ to see his device—that's over $5 today. It wasn't long before Wall Street was a tangle of telegraph wires. The telegraph turned New York into America's financial capital by eliminating the need for regional markets in other cities. The **stock ticker** was the next innovation created in 1867 by **Thomas Edison**. The ticker printed telegraph signals on a narrow paper tape—the **ticker tape**—that carried current prices to brokers throughout the nation. For the first time since the Buttonwood Agreement, people outside the exchange knew what was going on in the stock market. On Wall Street, "**bulls**" became the term for people who expect stock prices to rise. Alternatively, "**bears**" were those who anticipated drops in the market.

THE FIRST ECONOMIC EXPANSION

America's westward expansion detonated an explosion of trading activity and technology that sped up the pace of business beyond anyone's wildest dreams. The markets were unregulated by the federal and state governments and Wall Street was (and still is) no place for amateurs. The bulls included colorful characters like **Hetty Green**. The woman's severe appearance and miserly character earned her the nickname "the witch of Wall Street." Hetty, bitter from being swindled out of her inheritance by an insensitive male-dominated court system, eventually became the world's richest woman by making shrewd investments in railroads. Hetty Green amassed a fortune of $100 million dollars by investing in railroad stocks and real estate. Throughout her life, she employed a crude system of investigation before making any investment. She personally went to persons known to be enemies of the company directors or sellers of real estate. A money-wise and tough woman, she learned everything she could about the competition, then bluntly confronted the company directors or property sellers and waited for a reply.

America's railroads were among the most ambitious engineering projects in world history. **Railroad stocks** fueled a new frenzy on Wall Street. Until the railroads, corporations trading on Wall Street were little more than family concerns that didn't need a lot of capital.[3] When the country needed to build a trans-national railroad, it had to assemble a lot of cash. At that point the stock market became very important.

In the crowd on the floor of the exchange lurked ruthless insiders that moved stocks up and down to suit whatever schemes they had invented to fool the public out of its hard-earned money. The most notorious bear began as a store clerk who later became the most despised foe of New York high society.

Jay Gould was one of the most detested speculators on Wall Street. He was called the "Devil of Wall Street" because he never cared about the best interests of the companies he acquired control of. He was a master inside manipulator. Gould was the king of the short-sell manipulation called the **long (bull) squeeze,** a technique to make money by driving the price of a stock down. Here is how this manipulation works.

Gould focused on companies with very high prices. He would persuade other investors to loan him their shares in return for a small rate of interest. He would do this in different ways so that investors could not tell who they were really loaning their shares to. He would then immediately sell the stock over the exchange for top dollar. Gould published vicious rumors about the company in

Tip: Learn to acquire stock of good companies at low prices as large corporate insiders do when the public is not paying attention. If you do this, you will most likely become one of the Wall Street success stories in the next bull market!

---

[3] Capital is any form of wealth that can be employed or is capable of being employed in the production of more wealth.

a newspaper he owned in order to drive the stock price down where he would buy it back dirt cheap. He then returned the worthless stock to the investors and paid the small amount of interest that he owed. In this way he sold high then bought back low. This does not break the one golden rule on Wall Street—"**buy low and sell high.**" His profit was the difference between the price received when he initially sold the stock and the price he later paid to buy the stock back. The fact that a company and its shareholders were ruined in the process was of absolutely no concern to Gould.

The bulls had their inside manipulators, too. Large individual shareholders or small groups of speculators would corner a stock by purchasing all of the shares outstanding that could be bought (known as the **float**) when prices were low. This was known as **cornering a stock**. They would then spread rumors designed to create optimism about the company's prospects. The share price skyrocketed because only a relatively few number of shares were left in the market to "float" in the public's hands. Public investors had no idea that they were really trading with a limited group of people. This made the share price highly sensitive to increases in demand because supply was restricted by the inside manipulators in control of the corner. When the investors or group of investors who had the "inside scoop" on the manipulation sold their stock, the price plummeted as all of the shares flooded the market. This increased the floating supply of the stock. Since the supply of the shares of stock increased faster than the demand, the share price of the stock dropped. For this reason, investors or managers who had special inside information that can be used to get an unfair edge on the public are called "**insiders.**" One of the better known public figures known to have cornered a stock was Dutch immigrant **Cornelius Vanderbilt,** nicknamed the "Commodore" because he started with ferry boats and ocean liners.

July 8th, 1889 marked a milestone for Wall Street when the first financial newspaper, *The Wall Street Journal,* was published and sold at newsstands for the price of 2¢ per paper—40¢ today. **Charles Dow** and **Edward Jones** raised the standard of financial journalism with the new publication. The most popular feature was the daily index of twelve stocks known as the **Dow Jones Industrial Average (DJIA)**. By analyzing the performance of key companies in the economy at that time such as American Sugar, U.S. Rubber and General Electric, the index became the principal stock market barometer.

The DJIA made sense out of what was perceived as chaos. In the daily jumble of "up an eighth and down a quarter", it was impossible to tell whether stock prices generally were moving up or down. With the industrial average you could keep an eye on the long-term trends and not be confused by the short-term static. The telegraph, the ticker and *The Wall Street Journal* were the most powerful tools that opened the world of stocks to the general public. The so-called **"curbstone brokers"** continued to make an alternative marketplace for stocks—outside on the street curb—until they formed the **American Stock Exchange (AMEX)** in the 1920s. The bull and bear struggle made Wall Street dangerous to the public's financial health. Every 20 years or so, Wall Street would jam with investors panicked over a crash in prices. Sometimes the exchange was forced to close for days on end. The outbreak of World War I closed the stock market for more than 4 months.

J.P MORGAN

The most powerful man in America—the son of a prominent banker—made his mark in history as the undisputed king of corporate mergers. His name was **J.P. Morgan**. Morgan combined hundreds of companies into coast-to-coast monopolies. Morgan's crowning achievement came in 1901 when nine companies joined forces to become U.S. Steel. The merger made **Andrew Carnegie** the richest man in the world. It was the world's first billion-dollar corporation with stock so valuable that it boosted the DJIA by 500%! Andrew, who had arrived in America as a poor Scottish immigrant, used his wealth to create the U.S. public library and community college systems, single-handedly making education accessible to all. Bill Gates is following Carnegie's example today.

J.P. Morgan was a stern, autocratic man who never gambled. He based his decisions on business fundamentals and a company's susceptibility to stock manipulation. To protect his favored customers, Morgan insisted on a role in managing every company he created. If he sold you a stock in a railroad company and the railroad company got into trouble, he would move in and try to improve the situation personally.

Morgan controlled 341 seats on the boards of more than a hundred different companies. Investors respected Morgan, yet the public did not. His railroad monopoly raised shipping prices, hurting farmers. He supported child labor and opposed unions. President **Teddy Roosevelt** created antitrust regulations to bust up parts of Morgan's empire.

Morgan created no industries and produced very little economic wealth. He latched onto industries other men and women created and learned the trick of sharing that wealth with others he favored. J.P. Morgan was an adept inside manipulator. John Flynn in his book *Men of Wealth* describes how:

> *"The House of Morgan when putting out an issue of stocks could allot a few hundred or a few thousand to exalted persons who were useful to them. Then, when the shares were listed and manipulated into good prices for distribution on the Exchange, these preferred persons*

would reap swift, handy and rich profits, usually without putting up a cent."[4]

UBS Attorney Carlos Pou listens as Bill Garner, M.D. and CEO Dave Watkins discuss pharmaceutical and tech startups as seed investments.

The scope of Morgan's monopoly was staggering. Justice Brandeis in his book *Other People's Money* describes it's inter linkages:

> "*J.P. Morgan (or a partner), a director of the New York, New Haven & Hartford Railroad, causes the company to*

---

[4] The **inside corner** of a stock issue was well known by market participants to occur even prior to the great crash of 1929. The process of buying up a stock issue at a very low price from an unsuspecting public was known as "accumulating a stock" while dumping the same stock later on an eager public at frenzied high prices was referred to as "distribution of the stock." Some members of the public learned to spot price activity on long-term charts that indicated that a corner was starting. Today, insiders use stock options to achieve the same purpose as described in numerous publications including Maggie Mahar's book *Bull* and Arthur Levitt's book *Take on the Street*.

*sell J.P. Morgan & Co. an issue of bonds. J.P. Morgan &
Co. borrows the money with which to pay for the bonds
from the Guaranty & Trust Company, of which Mr. Morgan (or a partner) is a director. J.P. Morgan & Co. sell
the bonds to the Penn Mutual Life Insurance, of which
Mr. Morgan (or a partner) is a director. The New Haven
spends the proceeds of the bonds in purchasing steel rails
from the United States Steel Corporation, of which Mr.
Morgan (or a partner) is a director. The United States
Steel Corporation spends the proceeds of the rails in
purchasing electrical supplies from the General Electric
Company, of which Mr. Morgan (or a partner) is a director. The General Electric Company sells supplies to the
Western Union Telegraph Company, a subsidiary of the
American Telephone and Telegraph Company (AT&T);
and in which either Mr. Morgan (or a partner) is a
director. The American Telephone and Telegraph Com-
pany has an exclusive wire contract with the Reading
Railroad, which Mr. Morgan (or a partner) is a director.
The Reading Railroad buys its passenger cars from the
Pullman Company, of which Mr. Morgan (or a partner)
is a director. The Pullman Company buys (for local use)
locomotives from the Baldwin Locomotive Company, of
which Mr. Morgan (or a partner) is a director. The Reading, the General Electric, the Steel Corporation and the
New Haven, like the Pullman, buy locomotives from the
Baldwin Company. The Steel Corporation, the Telegraph
Company, the New Haven, the Reading, the Telephone,
the Telegraph, and the General Electric companies, like
the New Haven, buy steel products from the Steel Corporation. Each and every one of the companies named
markets its securities through J.P. Morgan & Co.; each
deposits its funds with J.P. Morgan & Co.; and with the
funds of each, each firm enters upon further operations."*

When Morgan died in 1913, he received a funeral befitting of royalty. The stock exchange closed for two hours as his hearse slowly paraded by. News of the death made the front page of newspapers around the world, but editorials were polarized. Some eulogies glorified Morgan; others vilified him. Some hated Morgan so intensely that his company became the target of a terrorist bombing seven years after his death.

On December 20th, 1920, a wagon loaded with explosives killed 30 people and injured more than 100. The entrances to the Morgan Company and the New York Stock Exchange across the street were littered with bodies. The crime was never solved but resulted in the formation of the **Federal Bureau of Investigation (FBI)**.

THE SECOND ECONOMIC EXPANSION

Wall Street quickly recovered from the 1920 blast but more shocks were ahead—the 1995 Oklahoma City bombing is just a continuation of such acts on U.S. soil. Unbeknownst to all, the biggest market boom in history was approaching as was the biggest crash. America had never seen anything like the roaring 1920s. The First World War ended in victory. Factories were booming and families had money to burn. By the 1920s the NYSE, a private institution, looked more architecturally impressive than government buildings. The exchange demolished the coffee house at the turn of the century to construct a larger structure that projected an image of strength and respectability. The new trading floor was gargantuan. Each stock was now traded at a special spot called a **post**. Steel stocks were clustered at one post; rail stocks at another.

The auctioneers, now called **specialists**, controlled the building, intermediating between brokers who represented buyers and sellers in the public. When a sale was made, **clerks** would rush the details of the transaction by pneumatic tube to the ticker tape room where typists hurriedly relayed the news to the world. In the post-war 1920s, the exchange was a place of glamour and wonder. Stocks became a national pastime in much the same way as they did in the 1990s.

Dr. Brown invites Michael Tennenbaum, friend and partner of billionaire John Paulson to talk with UPR-RP MBA students.

The public was fascinated by new inventions that led to exciting new products that Americans marched into retailers in droves to buy. Americans bought millions of radios and shares in the company that made them. They reasoned that the popularity of the wireless would drive up the share price of the manufacturer—Radio Corporation of America (RCA). As cars became popular so did automobile stocks. The demand for auto stocks pushed prices through the roof. Between 1924 and 1929, the DJIA shot up more than 300%. The bull market also attracted people who knew nothing about stocks, but who thought they were going to make some very quick money. The naïve and inexperienced public unknowingly made a market for the insiders as they were efficiently ushered into the slaughterhouse by Wall Street.

THE GREAT DEPRESSION

To experienced investors, the market was obviously over-blown. Yet unscrupulous brokers made matters worse by pressuring inexperienced investors into buying questionable stocks at high prices. Even more dangerous, many investors bought stock on credit, known in the trade as **"buying on margin."**

Banks were universal as they are in Europe today—offering a full menu of financial products including stocks. Stock brokerages competed directly with banks in those days. Bankers were allowed to represent their clients as stock brokers and looked at margin as they would any other loan. If you were a good client, you could buy a stock for as little as a 10% margin. If you wanted to buy a share of a $100 stock, you could put up $10 and the stock itself became collateral for the loan of the other $90.

The widespread use of credit and the tremendous rise of stock prices had experienced investors wondering how long the good times could last. Even the larger brokerage houses were growing concerned. In 1928, stockbroker **Charles Merrill** of the firm Merrill Lynch sent a clear warning to clients: *"Now is a good time to get out of debt. We do not urge that you sell securities indiscriminately, but we do urge in no uncertain terms that you take advantage of the present high prices and put your own financial house in order."*

His sage concerns were prophetic. Disaster struck Wall Street in October of 1929. The buying frenzy quickly disappeared. Hypothetical causes included consumer spending and sales of big ticket items having hit a slump—this was thought to cause several key stocks to decline. Once these critical security prices began to fall, speculators specializing in shorting stocks called **plungers** stepped in and drove the market down even more.[5] Short is a term meaning **short selling**. This is the sale of a security made by an investor who does not actually own the stock. The **short sale** is made in expectation of a decline in the price of a stock. If the stock price drops, it allows the investor to buy the shares back at a lower price in order to deliver the stock earlier sold short.

More selling caused more price drops. The drop sparked a flood of **margin calls** where brokers and bankers demanded that investors put more cash into their stock investing accounts. This was the very real risk of buying stock on credit. When a stock shrinks in price it is no longer valuable enough to be collateral for the loan. Investors must put up more cash, called **margin**, to even the scales. If they don't feed more cash into their account it is liquidated. On **October 24th, 1929,** thousands of investors could not raise the necessary cash by the time their brokers entered the exchange. When the opening bell rang on the NYSE at 10:00 AM, the equity fire sale began.

The public credit binge that had built up in the market was suddenly eating through it like the plague. The preponderance of sellers and buyers pushed all stocks lower forcing margin calls on even more investors and additional account liquidations. So many shares were sold so quickly that the

---

[5] Don't confuse a plunger like Jesse Livermore with a short squeeze manipulator like Gould. Livermore simply sold short lots of stock when he felt prices were excessive.

ticker ran four hours late. Thousands of investors rushed into the financial district desperate for news.

Suddenly there was hope. **Richard Whitney**, vice-president of the NYSE, met with top U.S. bankers and then marched onto the trading floor. He boldly bought 10,000 shares of U.S. Steel at $200. Whitney bought $20,000,000 worth of stock in just minutes. It was a powerful symbol, yet few knew that Richard Whitney was not trying to save the market but to fool it so that the banks could eventually sell out at a better price. Once again, Wall Street insiders showed their lack of concern for the small investor.

His triumphant stand stopped the panic temporarily but the sickening downward spiral of prices returned the following week with a bigger crash that continued for the next three years. Looking up from the bottom the drop was staggering. General Electric tanked from $1,612 per share in 1929 to $154 in 1932. General Motors spiraled from $1,075 in 1929 to $40 in 1932. The Dow plummeted 89% and $72 billion of investments were wiped out.

People lost their life savings on Wall Street. Leading economists of the day, including **Philip Fisher** of Yale, contended that the stock market crash alone did not induce the Great Depression that followed, but the public blamed Wall Street anyway. The panic terrified the public and as everyone stopped spending money the economy ground to a halt.

The crash revealed to economists major flaws in the United States' unregulated market for stocks. With the nation in financial ruin, the federal government began to impose radically far-reaching changes in the way the exchange did business. President **Franklin Roosevelt** was elected in 1932 as a reformer. In his very first speech in office, he blasted the stock market as he shouted, *"There must be a strict supervision of all banking and credit and investments. There must be an end to speculation with other people's money."*

On his second day in office, the president closed the NYSE for a week. He then pushed through Congress the most sweeping set of financial reforms ever enacted in the United States of America. Banks could no longer gamble savers deposits on stocks. Brokers had to act responsibly by treating their customer's money as if it was their own. Corporations that offered stock to the public were forced to file annual financial reports with the federal government.

These controls were intended to lessen the public view that Wall Street was nothing more than a "den of thieves". The stock market came back as a popular form of investing. Now president of the NYSE, Richard Whitney spoke out forcefully against the new regulations claiming that the stock market could police itself. This did not halt Roosevelt's push for federal oversight.

Roosevelt created the **Securities and Exchange Commission (SEC)** to enforce nearly all of the new rules. The SEC's first chairman was **Joseph Kennedy**. The SEC would eventually indict more than 300 people, including **Jesse Livermore,** famous for his short selling "plunging" of the market, in an effort to clean up Wall Street, but the agency found it virtually impossible to win convictions. The only insider to do jail time would be Richard Whitney himself, convicted of embezzlement.

The man who led the market during its deepest crisis spent three years in **Sing Sing prison** before being released. The newly reformed market was a lackluster place in the 1930s and 1940s as a shell-shocked public stayed away. Thousands of Wall Street workers lost faith in the paper chase and quit their financial professions.

THE THIRD ECONOMIC EXPANSION

Fact: The price of a memership "seat" on the NYSE in 1817 was $25. In 2000, it was over $1 million!

During World War II, it was not the stock market but the federal government that generated most of the money to reinvigorate U.S. industry. The stock market produced less than 20% of the capital needed to fuel the allied war machine and the federal government pitched in the rest. The war did, however, bring a historic milestone to Wall Street when women—until then restricted to work in the back rooms—now appeared on the stock exchange floor, ending a male-only tradition that had lasted 150 years.

With victory over German and Japanese axis forces appeared the stock market's most unique contribution to the war effort—mountains of ticker tape confetti welcoming home America's battle-weary troops. The baby boom years that followed World War II sparked the most recent major expansion of the U.S. economy. Unlike the 1920s, however, this boom was fueled by solid investing instead of speculation as the war-torn world economy healed and grew. Leading the charge was Charles E. Merrill who opened hundreds of new **Merrill Lynch** offices in the suburbs catering to a growing middle-class America. Merrill Lynch aggressively offered investment classes for women and placed a "How to Invest" exhibit in New York's central station. Commuters could check in to see if stocks were right for them. One of their innovations was to make analyst research reports free to Merrill Lynch clients as well as interested prospects.

The market fully recovered as American investors returned to stocks. In 1958 the Dow broke 300, the mark it had set 25 years earlier just before the 1929 crash. One of the most influential financial innovations of the '50s came not from Wall Street, but from a university campus 800 miles to the west of the trading floor. Economist **Harry Markowicz** at the University of Chicago developed the **theory of stock diversification** that became the rally cry for investment pools now called mutual funds.

Investors, he said, should remain continually invested in a wide range of stocks to reduce the risk of loss when a single company goes under. The concept of a diversified portfolio is a basic tenant of modern investment, legitimizing mutual funds that were notorious for fraud in the 1920s when they were called **investment pools**. This concept was so radical in the 1950s, however, that it eventually earned professor Markowicz the Nobel Prize in economics.

A financial mind that I greatly respect, **Warren Buffett**, considers Markowicz's theory nothing more than, *"an excuse for not thinking."* Specifically, he says, *"The strategy we've adopted precludes our following standard diversification dogma. 'Many pundits would therefore say the strategy must be riskier than that employed by more conventional investors. We disagree. We believe that a policy of portfolio concentration may well decrease risk if it raises, as it should, both the intensity with which an investor thinks about a business and the comfort-level he must feel with its economic characteristics before buying into it."*[6] At the height of the recent bull market, he said, "diversification is a substitute for thinking." Warren Buffet also said, *"Many in Wall*

---

[6] 1993 Berkshire Hathaway Chairman's Letter to Shareholders

*Street - a community in which quality control is not prized - will
sell investors anything they will buy."[7]*

Portfolio diversification was protective in the recent crash
from 2000 to 2003 and that of 2008 for those investors who
did not escape to cash. In the decades that followed, there
were downturns in the stock market. In the 1960s, there were
major slumps prompted by bad news during the President
Kennedy years and setbacks during the **Vietnam War**. The
OPEC oil embargo is thought by some to have hurt stock
prices in the 1970s as Americans waited in line for a gallon of
gas. The most dramatic event since the 1929 crash, however,
was the introduction of the computer.

A different kind of crash hit Wall Street in the 1960s – a paper
crash. The rise of pension plans and mutual funds pumped
trading volume to 11 million shares per day, yet every transaction was still processed by hand. There were mounds and
mounds of papers on desks with clerks just moving slips
back and forth. When the stock market had a lot of trading
volume it also had a paper crisis.

For brokerage companies, the paper crunch was devastat-
ing. Exhausted clerks were incapable of balancing the books
each night. The New York Stock Exchange had to close every
Wednesday to give the clerks a chance to catch up. The clerks
would work around the clock, every so often going to a cot
to sleep for an hour—sometimes they wouldn't go home for
weeks.

In 1968, at its height, trading volume across the exchange
touched off a **paper crunch** which forced nearly a hundred
brokerage companies into insolvency. Computers soon

---

[7] 2000 Berkshire Hathaway Letter to Shareholders

solved the problem with their ability to document market transactions at the speed of light. Since the 1970s, computers have assisted brokers with every aspect of the securities profession.

Computers routed smaller transactions directly to the trading posts, ending the delay caused by hand delivering an order across the trading floor. Computers vastly improved the market's ability to handle the ever growing volume of stock market trades. Computerization, however, also has a dark side.

Tip: Buy into the stock market while shares of good companies are selling at dirt cheap prices after sell-offs such as in 2003 and 2009.

Computers are thought by some financial economists to be responsible for the single biggest one-day price drop in stock market history. On **October 19th, 1987,** the market began an out-of-control decline that came to be known as "**Black Monday.**" Lightning fast computers had been programmed to instantly sell stocks when prices hit a pre-determined level.

The Dow plunged 508 points—a trading session drop of 23%. The precipitous drop with no unusual news foreshadowing the event taught stock traders a vital lesson that the market will crash when least expected. The stock exchange has since installed a series of so-called "circuit breaker" programs that restrict selling when the Dow fluctuates too rapidly to prevent such runaway disasters in the future.

A computer named **NASDAQ** in Connecticut brought the stock market to a historic crossroad in 1971. The NASDAQ system became a quick and inexpensive way to trade without the need for face-to-face interaction. NASDAQ links hundreds of brokerages worldwide. The NASDAQ system was the first network to allow people to trade electronically in smaller, generally "high technology" stocks.

The success of the NASDAQ system has led many financial economists and industry practitioners to question the future of trading floors such as that of the New York Stock Exchange where shares of large, more established corporations are bought and sold in traditional weekday auctions. Some financial economists strongly believe that the days of face-to-face transactions are numbered. Officials of the New York Stock Exchange defensively maintain that there are advantages to their time-tested ways of doing business. Only time will tell.

Most important of these supposed advantages is the role of the 450 specialists on the floor of the exchange who act as referees between the 900 brokers. The specialist occasionally buys and sells stock out of his or her own inventory to ensure that the market keeps functioning during periods of crisis. But they have their share of critics. Specialists have been accused of gouging an unfair profit from the public with their special inside command of market mechanics.

Two other recent innovations transforming the stock marketplace are the internet and online discount stock brokerages. Investors now have round-the-clock access to the buying and selling of equity securities worldwide.

Past dramatic increases in stock prices have roughly mirrored economic expansions, initially from the development of the railroad and westward expansion of the country, then during two post-world war peace times.

Puerto Rico Secretary of Commerce and Economic Development Alberto Bacó Bagué, CPA, JD is a prestigious alumnus of both the UPR-RP law and business schools. Secretary Bacó supports Dr. Brown's efforts to enhance the financial education of UPR-RP MBA students.

We are experiencing the greatest economic expansion in history as we leap into the communication age. The recent fall of the **Soviet Union**, with the highest average level of education of any populace, has added over a quarter of a billion brilliant minds to the world economy. **China** is also undergoing integration into the world marketplace, albeit on its own terms. These recent factors foreshadow a fourth massive global economic expansion. I believe that this may well allow the Dow Jones Industrial Average to eventually trade at the **100,000** level by the year 2050. Stock trends now circle the globe 24 hours a day from the United States to Tokyo to Europe and back again. In the U.S., stocks generate tens of billions of dollars per year to get new corporations started and to help old ones expand. The stock market puts the capital in capitalism. If you can learn to think independently and find what is uniquely yours, you can put it to work for you!

Chapter 2: What are Capital Markets and Why Are They So Important?

My brother and I grew up with John who was a year or two ahead of us in high school. My brother was a year behind me. When he graduated, the three of us decided to backpack throughout Europe. If you are in your 20s and reading this, I strongly recommend that you save some money, buy a backpack and a Eurail pass, and fly over for four to six months—it will be one of the best experiences of your life.

In six months, we visited over 40 countries, including Norway. At one point in our adventure, we were on a train that wound over the Norwegian mountains from Oslo and down to the scenic town of Bergen, which is situated inside a fjord. A fjord is a deep ocean inlet that is a submerged U-shaped valley carved out by glacial action. The fjord is characteristic of the coastal regions of Norway and they are spectacularly beautiful. The best way to understand a fjord is to imagine California's Yosemite Valley with the ocean filling the bottom.

The train tracks on the way down to Bergen are hacked out of the sheer granite walls of the fjord. To get a sense of the experience, imagine a train coming down the sheer vertical cliffs of the Yosemite Valley! I was sitting inside looking out the window at the impressive view when, suddenly, my brother sat down next to me. He was pale and trembling—an unusual state for my fearless brother. *"What's wrong, Todd?"* I asked. What he recounted was both terrifying and heroic.

Todd and John decided to walk out onto one of the platforms that connected the train cars. A train's cars are designed to be disconnected from one another and because of this, the railings between them are not only flexible but also latched, not bolted, in place. Todd and John looked down into the valley over 500 feet below. The view was mesmerizing – like hanging off the middle of a cliff in Yosemite. As Todd relaxed and leaned on the flexible railing connecting the cars, it snapped off! My brother began to fall forward off the platform when he felt a strong tug on the back of his jacket. It was John who, with a cool head, calmly grasped the door handle to one of the cars and quickly reached out and saved my brother's life!

The reason John was able to take the time and had the spare money to take the trip with my brother and me was that his family was very successful in the stock market. John related to me: *"My grandfather was involved in Wall Street with his firm. During World War II my father was a pilot and went to work with my grandfather when the war ended. My grandfather later died in a plane crash, but my dad worked with him quite a bit in the investment banking business before the accident. This was back in the early '50s."*

I asked John, "So your grandfather was in the business of taking companies public through IPOs?"

Tip: Understanding the herd behavior of the public can make you rich in the stock market!

John replied, *"Yes. My dad was involved in that business to a limited extent and then he moved to the West Coast and worked for a firm called David Skaggs, which was subsequently acquired by American Express. My dad traded stocks while he was involved with*

David Skaggs for a number of years. After my grandfather was killed in the plane crash, he did not want to have anything more to do with the stock business because it reminded him of the loss of his father—my grandfather. My father's painful memory of the loss of his father made it difficult for him to carry on with the securities business. He decided to move to a remote mountain valley in Northern California and was no longer involved in the day-to-day activities of David Skaggs. He bought our elegant mountain river ranch to engage in his passion of fishing and hunting to forget and ease the pain of the loss of my grandfather."

I asked John, "I know that your family became wealthy on Wall Street…didn't the big money come later with a massive trade your dad made in WD-40?"

John replied, *"I don't recall exactly how he became aware of the product – through active use of the product or through a tip from his contacts in the securities industry. I do know that he bought the stock shortly after it became public. All I know is that he bought the stock on the pink sheets at a very good price when it was on the OTC as a penny stock. He did really well with WD-40."*

Well indeed, John's grandfather and father did so well in the stock market that a trust fund now exists that is large enough to support not only their grandchildren, but their great-grandchildren in their lifestyle needs.

Capital markets make it easy for companies that need money to expand their production of consumer demanded goods and services. These markets help people in the public get their savings into investments that store their wealth. Hopefully, the public's investments grow bigger to create financial security over time. The process of transforming people's savings into investments creates the injection of money that corporations need to make more goods and offer more services that we all need.

For instance, I have a General Electric air conditioner here in my office as I write this. General Electric is such a big company that it is a Dow stock. General Electric offers bonds and shares of common stock for the public to buy through our capital markets. This allows some people in the public to save each month and buy GE stock or bonds. The money the company got from selling the stocks or bonds was used by GE to create the factory that produced the air conditioner that I bought at Costco and is now in my office.

When people retire or are short on cash, they can sell the stock or bonds and use the money as they choose. Some people have done so well in the stock market from wise investments that they have been able to retire early because they no longer have to worry about money. In this way, there is a vital "**circular-flow**" of capital, goods and services between individuals, households and corporations that has created the vast abundance of conveniences we take for granted today.

I had the enormous good fortune to travel behind the Berlin wall on our Euro-adventure in 1981, before the Soviet Union collapsed. The food and beer were the best I have ever had, and cost only pennies. But at the same time, I observed a populace in fear for its life, struggling to get by. People would avert their gaze when police cars would drive by. For all of the glitz and glitter of East Berlin as a showplace attempt to convince Westerners that a command economy worked, it was clear that everyone suffered except those at the top of the communist party.

The system in place at the time was a communist party ruled command economy based on the misguided sophist writings of **Karl Marx**.[8] "Doctor" Marx was an adulterer, a slothful, disheveled, lazy man. He was also an unremarkable thinker, an angry, egotistical anarchist with a big mouth. An arrogant and selfish hedonist who abused his family, he purchased his doctorate degree by mail from a German diploma mill.[9] The fact that some people take his confused ramblings seriously even today underscores the ease with which a socially savvy individual can manipulate the public with outright misrepresentations.

From this experience, I became obsessed to understand why some countries with high living standards in Western Europe, Asia and Northern America experienced abundance that allowed middle-class citizens to enjoy conveniences that medieval kings could not. I have long studied why command economies controlled by tyrannical political groups, churches or dictators force poverty on nearly all of its citizens.

I have since come to understand that healthy capital markets— like the U.S. stock and bond markets—are key to economic abundance in any country. Command economies do not have capital markets that allow individual citizens to participate in the economy as lenders (by buying bonds) or investors (by buying stock). This also means that there is no connection in command economies between what goods and services consumers really need and want and the existence of companies to provide those goods and services. Another grave flaw of a command economy is the odd psychological human quirk

---

[8] **A command economy** is an economy that is planned and controlled by a central administration, as in the former Soviet Union.

[9] **A diploma mill** is an unaccredited institution that grants fraudulent higher education degrees for a nominal fee without ensuring that students or professors are properly qualified.

that unprotected communal property is not valued. The only system that works is one that allows workers to selectively invest in stocks, lend their savings in the form of bonds or even abstain from participation in the capital markets if they so choose. People must at least perceive that if they play their cards right they have a shot of making it big.

Trap: Do not open a self-directed retirement account like a Standard or Roth IRA at a bank. They will try to force you to put your money into certificates of deposit (CDs) at a low rate of return so that they can lend it out at a high rate of return for their benefit, not yours. Open your IRA at an online stock brokerage.

This is also why the Soviet Union had some parts of their economy that were competitive on a worldwide scale, but due to inefficient distribution of resources and low worker productivity, most sectors of their economy were so inefficient that the population suffered.[10] Examples of exceptional product quality are AK-47 assault rifles produced by Russia, vaccines produced by Cuba and basic education in both. At the same time, however, the public in both countries suffered (or in the case of Cuba still suffers) from a lack of variety and distribution of even basic foodstuffs.

This is important to understand because, when you become a stock investor, you really are voting with your wallet. You are participating in markets that allow some countries in our world to experience standards of living unprecedented in recorded history. Some of the problems I discuss in this book,

---

[10] Capital is defined as cash money or goods used to generate income either by investing in a business or income producing property.

such as employee stock options and corporate insider special interest groups in Washington, undermine the integrity of our capital markets and need correction. Some of the quirky behavior of the public, on the other hand, like herd buying and selling, can make you rich if you know how to play the game as I teach you.

BANKS, BONDS, AND STOCK

To understand the capital markets, including the stock market, you must understand how companies get money to get started. It all starts with someone who gets an idea for a product or service that nobody has thought of. Imagine that a woman has a brilliant new idea for a product that everyone needs. Let's say she dreams up a new bicycle seat that is more comfortable and safer than any before. These people are called **entrepreneurs**. An idea in itself is worth nothing because the entrepreneur needs capital to buy patents, build a factory, push the product through the wholesale or retail supply chain, and market it so that consumers know about it. All of this is very costly and exhaustingly time-consuming without the stock market.

The first thing the entrepreneur could do is start a very small business with her savings and sell the bicycle seats locally. If they start to sell like hot cakes, she knows she can make a lot of money if she had a lot of bicycle seats. She has a problem because she needs more money to expand production to fulfill the demand for the bicycle seats.

The next step she will probably take is to get a **bank loan**. The problem here is that banks are difficult to deal with. Bankers have rigid rules and require collateral plus other personal guarantees from the entrepreneur. In this way, she can grow her business, but the money has lots of strings attached to it.

Scott Brown, PhD, CEO Dave Watkins, Secretary Alberto Bacó, Daniel Hall, JD and Annie Mustafa, MBA discuss the future of financial education in Puerto Rico.

There are two other ways for her to get the money she needs, assuming her company has enough years of successful selling and good payment records to the bank and suppliers. The first way she can raise money (capital) for her company is to sell bonds. The second is to issue stock.

When she sells bonds what she is really doing is buying money directly from public investors instead of buying the public bank deposits through a banker. Bonds are just another type of loan, but the banker is cut out of the loop as the annoying middle man. The way bonds work is that she makes an interest payment to the people who buy her bonds instead of a bank. The price of money, called **interest**, is based on the going rate in the market when she sells the bonds to the public.

You probably know that you can get a loan for different lengths of time. The same goes with bonds. Bonds are sold in different payback lengths called **maturities**. For example, bonds can have maturities of 1, 5, 10, or 15 years. During the time from issuance to maturity, those who invested in the bonds are paid interest, generally quarterly (every three months). The very last payment includes the original amount of the bond. If our bicycle seat lady sells bonds and her company fails, then the bondholders will take any value left in the business in repayment for the investment in the bonds. If for any reason she cannot pay the bondholders their interest payments, they can force her into bankruptcy. Even so, money a company raises from bonds has fewer strings attached than bank loans.

Remember the Dutch East India Company? Financiers came up with an idea hundreds of years ago that allowed them to get money from investors off the hook for payments unlike bonds and bank loans. The entrepreneur in this example can issue shares of stock. She will get money from investors and give up some of her ownership, but as her company grows, so will her portion. If the company becomes successful, then the stock will become popular and rise in price. The initial investors who bought a lot of stock get rich.

There are many vocabulary words and definitions in this book. It is important for you to have a conceptual foundation in your mind. As a stock investor it is absolutely critical that you develop a strong vocabulary and understanding of the equity markets, including stocks, bonds, mutual funds, and options. I call this the language of stock investing. This tongue has four distinct dialects: the language of stocks, the language of bonds, the language of mutual funds and the language of options. If you understand the key concepts and terminology of these markets, you will be setting yourself up for success as a stock investor—it will be easier for you to see through the lies on Wall Street!

Chapter 3:   The Language of Stocks!

Equity security is the technical finance term meaning stock in a publicly traded company. When I write equity or equity security, it means exactly the same thing as stock. A **security** is defined in the dictionary as an evidence of debt (such as bonds) or evidence of property (such as stocks). **Equity** is defined in the dictionary as the monetary value of a property or business beyond any amounts owed on it in mortgages, claims, liens, etc. The **equity** in your home, for instance, is how much cash you would get if you sold your house.

When you sell a house, the buyer's lender pays off your current mortgage and any associated closing fees; you get whatever is left over. That is your homeowner's equity. Equity in a corporation is a similar concept because it is what the owners would get after all debts are paid. An equity security is evidence that you have a

Tip: A strong stock market vocabulary will help you learn and grow into a strong stock investor!

claim to whatever residual value would be left in a company if it were liquidated and all of its debts and any associated fees were paid. An equity security is simply a share of stock in a publicly traded corporation. When I refer to the **equity market** in this book I am referring to the stock market. When I refer to equity securities or equities in this book I am referring to stocks.

Stock may take many forms, but here are the two basic kinds. As the name says, **common stock** makes you an "owner in common" of the corporation. Owners of common stock are called **common stockholders.** This is the most "common" type of stock people invest in because it offers the greatest probability that it will go up a lot in price. The term common stock is an equity security that has no special dividend rights and has the lowest priority claim in the event of bankruptcy. This means that common stockholders who own common stocks probably aren't going to get a piece of the profit pie and are the last to get paid anything if the company goes belly up! As horrible as this sounds, you will discover that buying common stock is one of the best ways to grow wealthy in the United States today.

The second type of stock is called **preferred stock.** Owners of preferred stock are known as the **preferred stockholders,** and they get treated differently by the corporation. They get preferred treatment when it comes to receiving dividends or cash payouts if the company goes broke. The bondholders and banks still get paid first if the company goes bust, but preferred stockholders get paid before common stockholders if the **inside corporate executives** decide to spread a little of the profits around in the form of dividends.

Convertible securities are weird things that you buy as one security and can later convert into another if you want. Most convertible securities are preferred stock or corporate bonds that are convertible into the firm's common stock.[11]

---

[11] Firm is another fancy way of saying company. A corporation is the most highly organized form of company and can issue shares on a stock exchange if it gets big enough. A firm is defined in the dictionary as a company, concern, business or house.

COMMON STOCK

Common stock makes you a part owner of a corporation, but the last in line to get paid out of day-to-day profits. A fancy way to say this is that **common stock** is a basic ownership claim against a corporation. Think of this as the investors who have put up investment capital to get things going. It's exactly the same as if you decided to invest in the creation of a business in the town or city that you live in. The most important thing about common stock is that it is what we financial economists call a **residual claim** against the corporation's cash flows or assets. In other words, if the inside corporate managers mess things up completely and the company goes down the tubes, then common stockholders have a legal right to stick their hands out for repayment in bankruptcy court along with all the other people and firms who got the shaft...but common stockholders are last in line!

If the company goes bust and has to be "sold off"—another way of saying liquidated—common stockholders (owners) can't be paid until what is owed to the employees (wages), the government (taxes), the courts (judgments), short- and long-term creditors (bank loans), bondholders (long-term debt), and preferred shareholders (other owners) are all paid off. After these prior debts are paid in full, the common stockholders get whatever is left over—the **residual value of the firm**. Common stockholders may directly share in the company's profits, but the inside corporate managers get to decide if any profits get paid out. The residual claim nature of common stock means that it is more risky than a firm's bonds or preferred stock because these investors are last in line if something goes wrong.

Legally, common stockholders enjoy **limited liability**, meaning that their losses are limited to the original amount of their investment in common stock. Here's an example: the **Bhopal Disaster** of 1984 is considered by authorities to be the worst industrial disaster in history. It was caused by the accidental release of 40 tons of **methyl isocyanides (MIC)** from a **Union Carbide India, Limited (UCIL)** pesticide plant located in the heart of the city of Bhopal in the Indian state of Madhya Pradesh. UCIL was a joint venture between Union Carbide and a consortium of Indian investors.

The accident, which occurred during the early hours of December 3, 1984, produced heavier-than-air toxic MIC gas which rolled along the ground through the surrounding streets, killing thousands almost instantly. The gas also injured anywhere from 150,000 to 600,000 people; at least 15,000 of these innocents later died. Heads rolled at the corporate level in the aftermath but none of the common or preferred shareholders stood to lose more than the initial investment they made when they purchased the company stock. This is what limited liability means.

Limited liability means that the personal assets of a shareholder cannot be taken away to satisfy the obligations of the corporation. In contrast, a **sole proprietor** who owns a gas station is personally liable for all of the debts and losses of the gas station he or she owns. Given the obvious benefits of limited liability, it is not surprising that most large firms in the United States are organized as corporations and not as sole proprietorships. If you are thinking about creating a business, DO NOT create it as a sole proprietorship. A corporation

Fact: At least 8,000 people died the night of the Bhopal Disaster, and more than 30,000 total in the aftermath.

or a Limited Liability Company (LLC) is infinitely more favorable.

Common Stock Dividends

Inside managers, at their discretion, can make corporate payments of profits to the stockholders (the corporation's owners) in the form of **dividends**. Common stock dividends are not guaranteed, and a corporation does not get driven into bankruptcy if they don't pay them. Residual dividends, if any, are paid out of the firm's after-tax cash flows. Dividend paying stocks are nicknamed **income stocks** because dividends give investors a steady flow of money.

Usually though, inside executives have money earmarked for other uses in the company. Those uses increase the creature comforts of the executives, either directly or indirectly reducing the wealth of the shareholder. Alternatively, executives tend to put money in projects that increase short-term cash flows to try to run up the stock price so they can dump their employee optioned stock on the public. Corporate managers are not on your side as a stock investor, even though they try to seem so in shareholder reports they send to you. Dividends are a problem for the company anyway, so don't worry about not receiving them. **Dividend income** is taxable for most investors. Because of this, corporate profits are double taxed—once when the company pays the corporate income tax on its profits and once more when investors pay their personal income taxes.

Double taxation is one of the major problems with dividends. The corporation gets taxed on its profits and then stock investors have to pay tax on the dividend income. In this very real sense, a dollar of profit by the corporation gets taxed twice before the owner of the company, the stock investor, gets to use it. To avoid double taxation, a few investors buy **growth stocks,** companies that reinvest their accumulated earnings instead of paying dividends. The main point is that growth stocks don't pay dividends. The vast majority of investors buy growth stocks because they tend to go up in price a lot more and a lot faster than dividend paying "income" stocks. Double taxation is a poor excuse for corporate inside executives to retain company profits for their direct or indirect benefit.

Rudolph William Louis "Rudy" Giuliani discusses methods to reduce crime in Puerto Rico with a local DNA database.

Reinvestment of earnings allows the company to accumulate capital and grow faster than it otherwise might, hence the nickname "growth stock" for equity securities that don't pay dividends. As a firm's earnings grow, people expect its stock price to rise. Stockholders can, if they are right and the price increases, sell their stock and pay capital gains taxes on their profits. You have to be very careful in selecting a growth stock because earnings and stock price increases do not go hand in hand. Many people believe this Wall Street and ivory tower myth. The public believes that, as a company makes more profit, its stock price must go up, but don't you believe it—reality is not so simple. Some excellent stocks primed for a rise may show losses on their income statement for reasons I will later explain in the chapter on fundamental analysis.

The **Tax Reduction Act of 1997** set a lower tax rate on **capital gains** than on dividends.[12] The maximum tax rate on assets held for more than 18 months was lowered from 28% to 20%, and later to 15%. Note also that taxes on capital gains are paid only on realization of the gain when you sell. You can reduce your tax bill by delaying the sale of your stocks to postpone the realization of a capital gain. In other words, if you learn to invest for the long run, you will save a lot of money in taxes. For this reason, patience is an investor's great virtue in the stock market. This is important because the very high short-term capital gains tax rates will literally suck all of the profit out of the best short-term trading system. Actively seek ways to minimize taxes on your investments as aggressively as you seek capital appreciation.

---

[12] Capital gain is the amount by which an asset's selling price exceeds its initial purchase price. A **realized capital gain** is an investment that has been sold for a profit. An **unrealized capital gain**, also called a paper gain, is an investment that hasn't been sold yet but would result in a profit if sold. You do not pay taxes on paper gains. Capital gain is often used to mean realized capital gain. For most investments sold at a profit, including mutual funds, bonds, options, collectibles, homes, and businesses, the IRS is owed capital gains tax. A **capital loss** is just the opposite.

Common Stock Voting Rights

Even though stockholders own the corporation, they aren't managers of the business—they have no control over day-to-day business activities. They have no control over dividend payments even though they are the true owners of the firm. You would think they could simply say, *"Just pay me what is mine, Mr. inside executive manager!"* Today, control of the firm now rests firmly in the hands of inside corporate executives who are supposed to be concerned about the shareholder's financial welfare but rarely are.

Trap: Don't ever buy shares of stock simply because you are attracted to the company's product or some report about the quality of the company. Focus on buying stock in companies that, mysteriously, nobody seems to be paying attention to yet are rising on strong volume.

Shareholders exercise control over the firm's daily operations indirectly through a corporate board of directors. They do this by electing people called **directors of the board** who the shareholders believe will best defend their interests. The election of a board of directors is through shareholder **voting rights**. It is the task of the **board of directors,** on behalf of the owner shareholders, to keep a watchful eye on the corporate inside executives. Shareholders elect directors by casting votes at an annual meeting. In reality, this has its share of problems, because most shareholders cannot actually attend the meeting. They have to instead vote by **proxy** through absentee ballot or by endorsing a representative.

Here is how the all-important board of directors is supposed to be formed. There are two ways of electing directors: cumulative voting and straight voting. In **cumulative voting,** all directors are elected at the same time and the shareholders are granted a quantity of votes equal to the number of directors being elected times the number of shares owned. In most cumulative voting schemes, shareholders are permitted to distribute their votes for one director. The effect of cumulative voting is to give minority shareholders, those owning small proportions of the stock, a voice in the company's decisions.

With cumulative voting, minority shareholders are guaranteed to elect the largest percentage of directors. This is less than the percentage of shares that minority shareholders control. For instance, if five directors are being elected and the minority shareholders control 42% of the shares, they are assured of being able to elect two directors because each director requires 20% of the total votes cast to be elected. However, if only three directors are being elected, then the minority shareholders would be able to elect only one director because each director requires 33.3% of the total votes.

In **straight voting**, directors are elected one-by-one. Thus the maximum number of votes for each director equals the number of shares owned. Under this strategy, it is difficult for minority shareholders to obtain representation on the board of directors because any shareholder who owns even slightly less than 50% of the shares can elect the entire board of directors. It should be obvious why inside corporate executives love straight voting—they get more control of the board of directors away from the shareholders.

Normally, one vote is attached to one share of stock, but there are exceptions called **dual-class firms**. During the 1980s, many firms recapitalized with two classes of common stock that have different voting rights. **Recapitalize** is a fancy word for re-organizing the financing of the company. By issuing stock with limited voting rights compared to existing shares, the managers of a firm can raise **equity capital** (money) by selling stock and still maintain control of the firm.

They are able to maintain control because investors that buy the new shares can't vote, leaving the inside corporate executives to do what they want. Needless to say, dual-class firms are controversial. Many financial economists like me view **dual-class recapitalizations** as attempts by managers to entrench themselves (dig in like a tick, as they say in the south) so that they can unduly enrich themselves.

Corporate inside executives created dual class recapitalizations as a tool to chew more meat off of the bone than they deserve. Opponents of dual-class recapitalizations argue that *"managers of dual-class firms are insulated from the disciplining*

2004 Top 10 Most Highly Paid CEOs		
Yahoo Inc.	Terry S. Semel	$109,301,385
Coach Inc.	Lew Frankfort	$64,918,520
XTO Energy Inc.	Bob R. Simpson	$62,141,981
United Health Group Inc.	William W. McGuire	$58,784,102
Viacom Inc.	Summer M. Redstone	$56,017,985
TXU Corp.	John C. Wilder	$54,960,893
Countrywide Financial Corp.	Angelo R. Mozilo	$52,993,637
Occidental Petroleum	Ray R. Irani	$52,648,142
KB Home	Bruce Karatz	$47,288,228
Gateway Inc.	Wayne R. Inouye	$46,338,744

Source: **Executive PayWatch**

effects of the proxy or takeover process, through which ineffective managers can be replaced." Proponents—corporate lawyers on the payroll of insiders—say that managers of dual-class firms are *"free to pursue riskier, longer-term strategies that ultimately benefit shareholders without fear of reprisal if the short-term performance of the corporation suffers."*

Corporate Governance

As I mentioned before, investors have different likes and dislikes—some people like growth stocks and other people like income stocks. Yet other investors prefer bonds. A fancy way to say this is that investors have different **portfolio preferences**. Corporations have different growth opportunities depending on the age of the company, the industry and many other factors. Different corporations have different corporate strategies, for instance, deciding to emphasize growth by reinvesting profits or to pay profits out to the corporate owners by making dividend payments to the shareholders. The stock market is supposed to match investor desires with companies managed by like-minded strategizing corporate executives. If the executives don't do what they are supposed to because they are lazy or cheating the shareholders as owners of the corporation legally have the power to fire or penalize them.

That is all fine and dandy, but we have lots of **agency problems** in corporate America today where inside executive managers are sucking away as much value in the business from stockholders as they can in the form of perquisites, profits and employee stock option gifts. **Perquisites**, commonly known as "perks", are executive goodies that cost the corporation lots of money that should go to the shareholders. Lear jets, useless "business trips" in super expensive resorts even royalty can't afford, and overpaid supermodel secretaries are all examples of perquisites.

Executives throttle the companies they manage with **agency costs**. The doctoral-level finance literature describes two basic types of managerial inefficiencies that are both called **shirking**—a fancy way to say thievery or laziness. The first agency cost I want you to understand is **misfeasance**. The idea here is that if lazy inside corporate executives worked harder, were smarter, or were more careful they would earn more money for shareholders—if they hang out all of the time on the golf course they aren't exactly taking care of business. The second agency cost is **malfeasance**. Here, thieving inside executives cheat the corporation through lavish perks on themselves. The history of American public business corporations are filled with examples of both forms of **shirking**, ranging from congenital unluckiness (executives just born unlucky but, unfortunately for shareholders, in control of the company), to incompetence and, most commonly, to outright theft.[13] These agency problems are at the core of academic finance research in corporate governance.

This leads us to an area of finance that is very important for stock investors called corporate governance. We have many problems today with corporate governance. "*Corporate governance is concerned with holding the balance between economic and social goals and between individual and communal goals.*" The aim of corporate governance is to "*align as nearly as possible the interests of individuals, corporations and society.*"[14]

In other words, corporate governance is also the study of how to avoid a society where the rich get richer and the poor get poorer until the poor get fed up and revolt. The corporate governance framework is supposed to encourage the

---

[13] Shirking is defined as dodging or evading work, duties or responsibilities.

[14] Sir Adrian Cadbury in 'Global Corporate Governance Forum', World Bank, 2000

efficient use of resources and to require accountability for the **stewardship** of those resources.[15]

All our problems in corporate governance come from the fact that our large modern day corporations are no longer under control of the owner-shareholder, yet these non-owner managers control most of the world's wealth. The 30 companies that are in the Dow index control an enormous share of the world's profitable industrial production and an

Fact: CEOs exercising employee stock options drain millions of dollars each year from the capital needed to make American companies more competitive.

even larger share of the U.S. economy. Oppressive dictators around the world find themselves threatened by the U.S. federal government and military. Yet men who are able to climb to the top of corporate America and are astute enough to control the board of directors have a more profitable dictatorship without any fear of invasion. Our corporate dictators call the shots in our federal government to a large degree and have full support of a White House that projects the modern day corporate inside executive to be the poster person for the American Dream. Executive managers know that even if they do a little jail time for inside trading or stock manipulation, they will still come out wealthier than most of today's European royalty. Ask Martha Stewart.

Shareholders have been stripped of voice or control of the firm. Imagine how you would feel if you paid for a

---

[15] Stewardship is defined as the act of managing another's property or affairs; administering anything as the agent of another or others.

McDonald's franchise with your hard-earned savings. You are the owner and the manager is your employee. Now imagine how you would feel if the manager of your hamburger restaurant, who is really your employee, got to manage, take whatever cash, benefits, or do whatever they want without asking your opinion. How would you feel if you complained, pressed charges, or tried to fire them and found out your restaurant manager had the support of Congress and the Delaware "CEO Loving" Court?

The fact that there have been a lot of corporate scandals in large and once-respected companies proves that there is a lot of room for financial mischief inside U.S. corporations. Corporate inside executives have been caught in outright lies to shareholders and workers in such cases as **Enron** and **World-Com**. The inside corporate executives at **America Online (AOL)**, for instance, are notorious in corporate America for "cooking" their accounting books.

The problem of being ripped off by the managers of a corporation is not new. Economist **Adam Smith** in 1776 wrote, *"The directors of [joint stock] companies, however being managers rather of other people's money than of their own, it cannot be expected that they should watch over it with the same anxious vigilance [as owners]...Negligence and profusion, therefore, must always prevail, more or less, in the management of the affairs of such a company."* What Adam Smith so wisely said is that since the inside corporate executives get to control your hard-earned savings without risking a dime out of their pocket, some are going to waste your money on undeserved daily luxuries while stealing as much as they can.

Here is how inside corporate executives take control away from the shareholders. When a company is founded, the **balance of power** between shareholders and inside corporate executives is not a problem. This is because everyone in the small company understands that the **shareholders** are the owners. Inside corporate executives clearly understand that they are employees and work happily on reasonable wage and benefits as compared to rank-and-file. **Directors** view themselves as representatives of the shareholders. They know that it is their job to hire and fire and set the wages of the executive managers. In the beginning, there are only a few owners who are shareholders. These are generally the founding family or partners who started the company. Examples include the Ford family of **Ford Motor Company** or the Disney family of **Walt Disney Company**.

To summarize, a properly operating corporation has a **chief executive officer (CEO)** who is the top manager (employee) of the company. The **board of directors'** job is to hire the CEO and other officers and set their wages. The **directors of the board** are selected by the shareholders by democratic vote. The **chairman of the board** presides over all board meetings and recommends members of the board to the shareholders. What happens when the company grows larger and makes lots of money?

As the company grows, these relationships blur and the perfect family becomes dysfunctional. Growth is wonderful but requires more capital to keep it all going forward. The initial shareholders who are usually the founding family or partners have a limited amount of money they can put up and are normally tapped out from starting the company. They know that if they bring in other investors they can grow a lot more, so they sell shares to the public. This means that the **shareholder base** becomes very diverse, as lots of different people become owner-shareholders in smaller and smaller chunks as more stock is issued and sold. This is called **shareholder pool dilution**.

At this point, the company can take a number of different paths. Either the original founders continue to control the company or they decide to enter high society and hire a professional manager, with an MBA from a big-name school, as CEO, while controlling him or her through the board of directors with a firm hand. Alternatively, the family can maintain managerial control of the company. In the case of the Ford Motor Company, the founding Ford family still controls the company. Family members are groomed for upper management and if a corporate executive becomes too powerful, the family simply throws him or her out. This is exactly what the Ford family did when **Lee Iacocca** was tossed aside. This turned out to be an unwise move on the part of the Ford family. Iacocca turned Chrysler around from bankrupt to a major competitor of Ford today.

Trap: When mutual and hedge funds sell out, a stock is said to be "unsupported" and falls rapidly in price.

Another potential outcome is that an ego driven inside corporate executive, through corporate gamesmanship, gets appointed to both the position of chairman of the board and chief executive officer. At this point, the fox lives in the henhouse because the highest ranking employee of the firm can now appoint directors who will vote according to their own desires. This is exactly what happened when **Michael Eisner** gained control of the Walt Disney Company as both CEO and board chairman. He was able to completely lock the Disney family and all small shareholders out of the governance of the firm. Eisner ransacked the company for nearly $1 billion.

As the company expands and its financing needs grow, the average shareholder controls fewer and fewer shares of stock in the corporation. As this happens, corporate inside executives look at shareholders as irrelevant for input in managing the company daily. In short, since inside corporate executives can do what they want and can listen to shareholders less and less, the inside corporate executives become arrogant. Again, this happens because shareholders have to agree to give up some of their ownership to allow the firm to continue to grow. In doing so, however, they lose the key to the henhouse.

The cost of **active monitoring** of the performance of inside corporate managers becomes too expensive compared to what the shareholder earns from his or her relatively small ownership in the company at this point. Shareholders stop attending annual meetings and vote with management or throw the proxy in the wastebasket. Investors don't know enough to make an informed decision about who would be a good director. This is called **voluntary shareholder absenteeism**. When combined with strong and arrogant corporate insiders who have gained control of the company through the board of directors, it creates a problem that is at the heart of today's severe **corporate governance crisis**.

The important historical lesson is that the absentee shareholder system breeds severe arrogance on the part of corporate inside executives. This point will be even more evident when you read the chapter of this book describing historical corners. The crisis I am referring to is that you, as part owner of the firm, no longer have any voice whatsoever in the hiring and firing of top inside managers or the composition of companies' boards of directors. The "little guy" has been completely cut out of the loop in American corporate culture. It is not supposed to be this way, but it is, and it is supported at the highest levels of the federal government.

How is it that the top employee of the firm ends up controlling the very board of owners that is responsible for his or her hiring, firing and compensation? Corporate insiders argue that they should have input into the board of directors because the corporation has a "social responsibility" to groups other than the shareholders, which include debt holders and employees.

Governor Alejandro Javier García Padilla and Secretary Alberto Bacó Bagué discuss economic development in Puerto Rico through tax incentives.

Another typical inside executive defense offered is that the board requires the CEO and other management input to make proper decisions. CEOs use this argument to get onto the board to drive a wedge between the different forces in the company. What corporate executives never explain is why the CEO needs a vote on the board—let alone the chairmanship—to supply the board with his or her input. It takes a strong will to stand up to the CEO-chairman even for fully independent directors who are not part of the insider's web of cronies.[16]

In today's system, the vast majority of directors sit on boards because the CEO recommended them. The owner-shareholder never has input. As cronyism erodes the board's decision-making ability, the corporate executive insider is the clear winner. Michael Eisner could acquire nearly a billion dollars' worth of stock in the Disney corporation by simply asking a board of directors composed of his cronies to gift him all of the **employee stock options** he wanted. Shareholders were completely powerless to stop him because they had been eliminated from the process.

What few U.S. investors stop to ponder is the fact that it is now common for the CEO to also occupy the post of board chairman. Only recently has there been any debate among academics questioning this American tradition. Institutional shareholders, primarily mutual funds, and other governance activists, mainly unions, recommend separation of the roles. In Europe, the tradition has been not to place the CEO in the chair. In some countries of the **European Economic Union** this is enforced by statute.

The politically-driven widespread practice of placing insiders on boards appears to have started in 1976. Germany expanded its **co-determination law** from the political pressure of **worker unions**. The newly-expanded law required companies with more than 2,000 employees to give half of the supervisory board seats to employees. This created a

---

[16] Cronies are defined in the dictionary as close friends or companions; chums. Cronyism is where the inside chief executive officer who is also the chairman of the board appoints his buddies to the board of directors. The CEO can then pass whatever corporate rule he or she wants, including the gifting of more employee stock options to him or herself.

precedent that inside corporate executives in the U.S. were able to point to.

The Poison Pill

A **takeover bid** is a corporate action where one company, the acquiring company, makes a "bid" to buy another company, the target company. If the target company is publicly traded, the acquiring company will make an offer for the outstanding float of shares. A welcomed takeover usually refers to a friendly takeover that the inside corporate executives of the target company approve of. **Friendly takeover bids** generally go smoothly because both companies welcome it. In contrast, an unwelcome or **hostile takeover bid** can get downright nasty. One of the biggest reasons these takeover attempts are unwelcome is because the inside corporate executives of the target company are afraid they will be thrown out of the new combined company! Famous MIT Nobel Laureate economist **Paul Samuelson,** in his book *Economics*, explained, *"Takeovers, like bankruptcy, represent one of Nature's methods of eliminating deadwood."*

In the case of a **hostile takeover bid**, which would replace corrupt or incompetent inside corporate executives (deadwood), those very same executives today sit on a board with the power to stop the takeover and ignore the shareholder's best interests. United States courts have never recognized this as a problem or tried to fix it. Instead the Delaware Supreme Court has, over the past two decades, granted inside corporate executives broad power to ignore the right of owner-shareholders to organize a hostile takeover bid to get rid of lazy or thieving insiders. As a result, insiders have succeeded in blocking the rights of small shareholders who only want to sell their shares to someone else who is trying to accumulate a controlling block of the stock to do some managerial house cleaning.

A particularly effective inside corporate executive defense is the so-called "poison pill". This is a clause in the corporate charter that is triggered if any investor accumulates a 15% share of the company they are trying to take over. When this happens, all shareholders except the 15% block holder get to purchase new shares for an arbitrarily low price, such as half market value. This is like asking the block owner who is trying to clean out the bad management to pay a dividend to all the other shareholders, financed out of the block holder's personal wealth. Boards can issue poison pills right after receiving a hostile bid (this is called a "**morning after pill**").

An important 1985 decision was **Moran vs. Household International,** in which the **Supreme Court of Delaware** (where 60% of Fortune 500 companies are incorporated) upheld the inside controlled board's right to refuse to remove a poison pill, even though there was an all-cash offer on the table and the majority of the company's stockholders had already tendered their shares. The Delaware Supreme Court ruled that top employees have more rights than the owners of a public company. With this decision,

Fact: In the early days of Wall Street, stock merchants kept a physical inventory of securities on hand which they sold "over-the-counter" like any other retail product. Even today, with fully electronic transactions, NYSE market makers and NASDAQ brokerages are said to "carry inventory."

the federal government gave insider controlled boards, the vast majority of U.S. corporations, the right to ignore lucrative offers that are beneficial to the owners but not to managers.

The poison pill has been the sharpest tool for the executive corporate insider to pirate the public of its hard-earned savings. **Hostile takeovers** transformed lots of poorly managed and inefficient companies into well-oiled business machines from 1975 to 1985. The poison pill has completely stopped hostile takeovers in the United States—not one has gone through since 1985. Nobody dares take on the insiders today because they have everybody by the gonads.

As a stock investor, you should be concerned. The poison pill is a symbol of state sanctioned theft by insiders of the fundamental shareholder right to sell shares of stock to the highest bidder. Today, no takeover can proceed unless corporate insiders—who are the employees, not the owners of the firm—agree to remove the poison pill. Boards refuse to remove the poison pill because malfeasant executives know that they will lose their positions in the company.

To summarize, American executive corporate insiders (1) are excessively overpaid in terms of salary and employee stock options, (2) have control of the company that no employee should have, and (3) remain in control through the legislative support of the federal government that no government should provide. It is no wonder that the 1985 Delaware Supreme Court precedent has caused an era of governance decline into crisis in corporate America. The robber barons are back!

Institutional Activism

In the past three decades, the growth of pension funds and other investment pools such as mutual and hedge funds have grown massively as inside corporate executives have shifted workers' retirement funds into self-directed defined contribution plans like the 401(k). Investment funds control

50% of household stock market savings. These funds are now so large that they normally control 2% to 3% of the total equity of a company in which they purchase stock for the mutual fund's investors.

Some of these large investment pools are upset about the excessive state-sanctioned control that inside corporate executives enjoy over the boards they sit on. This has allowed the absentee shareholder to regain a voice on the board to some degree. Over the last ten years, they have been pushing for non-excessive executive compensation and the separation of the posts of CEO and board chairman.

For example, investors, with the Disney family in the lead, were able to force Michael Eisner to step down as chairman. The victory was bittersweet, however, because of the extensive ransacking that this insider had already done. Another example is the success of a shareholder resolution that led the drug giant Merck to refuse to offer Richard Clark, the new CEO, the chairmanship. Instead, the board took the unusual step of having a troika of directors acting as "chair."[17]

The way the CEO-chairman gets his or her cronies on the board is through the current election system. The company sends out the election ballot to all shareholders. When the shareholder receives the ballot, it has only two options, "yes" or "abstain". If every single shareholder but one abstains, the CEO-chairman gets the crony director he or she wants. Of course, they also get the lock-hold on setting their salary as well as the gifting of employee stock options to themselves through their "good ol' boy" board they have created. The

---

[17] A troika is defined as an association or a group of three.

SEC tried to change this by forcing corporations to allow shareholders to write in their candidates for directors.

Not surprisingly, the special interest lobbying group for American corporate executive insiders, the Business Roundtable, could buy support from congress and the SEC was forced by capitol hill to abandon the proposal. Arthur Levitt, as former head of the SEC, fought for nearly a decade to force inside corporate executives to report the gifting of employee stock options as a cost on the accounting books. To Levitt's bitter disappointment, the Business Roundtable succeeded in garnering support from Congress. Senator Joseph Lieberman, Al Gore's Vice-Presidential running mate in the 2000 elections, spearheaded the defense of excessive insider compensation. For more about this read Arthur Levitt's book *Take on the Street*.

Eisner's Disney is a prime example of poor corporate governance. The board of directors included Eisner's friends from actor Sidney Poitier, architect Robert A.M. Stern, who has designed many Disney properties, to former Senator George Mitchell, who consulted for Disney. The board's poor judgment was best seen in the obscene compensation packages it awarded him during his tenure as CEO.

Tip: The very best way to invest long-term in the stock market is through a Roth IRA and Roth Solo K!

In the spring of 2001, Forbes concluded that in the previous five years, Eisner had made $737 million. This was during a period when the company's profits fell and the stock had performed poorly.

Eisner made a lot of stupid business decisions, including a spat with Jeffrey Katzenberg, genius behind such movies as *Shrek*, who left, taking the big green ogre with him. He was also responsible for the hiring and firing of the grossly overcompensated Michael Ovitz, losing the Pixar deal (which went on to make a fortune), and triggering a revolt by Roy Disney and Stanley Gold. After Frank Wells died, there was nobody at Disney with the power or guts to say no to Eisner.[18] In large part, this is because Eisner was so good at stocking the board with ceremonial directors and, even worse, personal cronies. The board included such "luminaries" as Eisner's personal lawyer, his architect, and the principal of the elementary school attended by one of his children.

In 2002, reforms at Disney included changes to the board that led to corporate governance improvements. Yet Eisner managed to turn even those reforms to his advantage. Roy Disney, part of the original founding family and Walt Disney's nephew, was forced out by a mandatory retirement provision, which exempted former CEOs! The only other persistent Eisner critic on the board—Disney's ally Stanley Gold—was kept off key committees because his business dealings with the firm meant he did not qualify as an independent director under the 2002 reforms.

The long-term problem at Disney was that virtually every mechanism created to hold boards of directors accountable for their actions failed. Board of director independence to

---

[18] Previously, Wells had worked for Warner Brothers as its vice president in 1969, then in 1973 as president and in 1977 as vice chairman until he left the company in 1982. Disney shareholders Roy E. Disney and Stanley Gold recruited Wells to become Disney's second-in-command, under Michael Eisner, in their bid to oust CEO/President Ron W. Miller. Over time, Wells became very outspoken against Eisner's bad management.

act failed because the board was comprised of nominally independent folks who in fact were cronies of Eisner or "know-nothing" ceremonial directors. Shareholder activism failed because voting never made a serious dent in the board's complacency. Litigation failed because the board was willing to pay zillions to Ovitz, Katzenberg, and anyone else who sued. The Sarbanes-Oxley Act and other post-Enron reforms failed because Eisner was so good at boardroom politics that he could use even those reforms to further entrench himself in the company.[19]

Preferred Stock

Like common stock, **preferred stock** represents owner-ship interest in the corporation, but as the name implies, it receives "preferential" treatment over common stock with respect to dividend payments and a claim against the firm's assets in the event of a bankruptcy or liquidation. In liquida-tion, preferred stockholders are entitled to the issue price of the preferred stock plus accumulated dividends after other creditors have been paid but before common stockholders are paid.

Preferred Stock Dividends

Preferred stock is usually sold in terms of the dollar amount of its dividend. This dividend is different than a common stock dividend. With a common stock dividend, corporate inside executives can change the amount or arbitrarily decide

---

[19] The U.S. federal **Sarbanes-Oxley Act (SOX)** was created in 2002 to protect investors by improving the accuracy and reliability of corporate disclosures. The act covers such issues as establishing a public company accounting oversight board, auditor independence, corporate responsibil-ity and enhanced financial disclosure. The act came in the aftermath of a series of corporate financial scandals, including those affecting Enron, Tyco International and WorldCom (now MCI).

Ex-Prime Minister of Spain José María Aznar warns that there are no miracles in the path to economic recovery for Puerto Rico—growth will only arise from global investor confidence.

not to pay it. A preferred dividend is a fixed obligation of the firm—similar to the interest payments on corporate bonds which are also fixed payments.

Bonds are loans that the company has to pay back in principal and interest. The company makes a one lump repayment of the principal when the bond comes due and has to make interest payments every so often as per the terms of the bond. The key thing to understand is that a bond is a loan to the corporation made by investors while stock is ownership. A corporation will go into default for not making an interest payment on a bond but not for passing on making a dividend payment.

Most preferred stock is nonparticipating and cumulative. Preferred stock is **non-participating** in the sense that the preferred dividend remains constant regardless of any increase in the firm's earnings. Firms can decide, however, not to pay the dividends on preferred stock without going into default. Default is a fancy way of saying going bad on a loan. In other words, preferred dividends are not loan payments that corporations absolutely have to pay like they do when they sell bonds or go to a bank for money.

The **cumulative** feature of preferred stock means that the firm cannot pay a dividend on its common stock until it has paid the preferred stockholders the dividends in arrears. In other words, the dividends are supposed to be paid out quarterly, just like bond interest payments. If the firm cannot make the preferred dividend payment, the company still owes the dividends to the preferred shareholders if they can make them in the future. The company must pay the preferred shareholders before the common shareholders, and that is why they call them preferred. Some preferred stock is issued with adjustable rates. **Adjustable-rate preferred stock** became popular in the early 1980s, when interest rates were rapidly changing. The dividends of adjustable rate preferred stocks adjusted periodically to changing market interest rates.

Preferred Stock Voting

Generally, preferred stockholders do not vote for the board of directors. Exceptions to this rule can occur when the corporation is in arrears on its preferred dividend payments.

CONVERTIBLE SECURITIES

Convertible securities are important for you to understand, because they affect the float of common stock—the total common shares outstanding available for public purchase. As you will learn later in this book, when the float increases it has a tendency to depress the price of a common stock.

It can be very useful to know if there is a lot of convertible securities around that could be added quickly to the float of common stock. Sudden increases in the shares outstanding of a firm are one of the clues you will learn to look for that tell you insiders are bailing out at the top of a long extended upward price run—which should make you start to consider selling out as well.

Convertible preferred stock can be converted to common stock at a predetermined ratio (such as two shares of common stock for each share of preferred stock). By buying such a stock, you can get a good dividend return. If the common stock rises in price, your convertible preferred stock will increase in value because you can choose to convert your preferred stock into common stock if you want. If you do convert, however, you will not get any more preferred dividend payments.

Convertible bonds can be exchanged for shares of common stock. Until it is converted, it is corporate debt. The bond interest and principal payments are contractual obligations of the corporation that must be paid, or the corporation will go into default. Most convertible bonds are **subordinated debentures**, meaning that they get paid after other bonds if cash is tight in the corporation.[20] Investors who own convertible bonds have a lower ranking claim against corporate profits than most other debt holders, but their claim ranks higher than stockholders. Stockholders are at the bottom of the food chain when it comes to corporate profits, but are willing to take on this risk because of the possibility of

---

[20] Debentures are unsecured bonds that are only issued by creditworthy firms. Convertible bonds are almost always debentures and are also known as **unsecured junior bonds**.

potentially fantastic advances in stock prices. The increases in stock prices in the last century alone have made many American households rich—more so than any other investment market; futures, forex, bonds or real estate.

Because convertible bonds increase in value with rising stock prices and provide the fixed income and security of bonds, they are popular with investors, who are usually willing to pay more to acquire convertible over conventional bonds issued by the same corporation. From the corporation's point of view, convertible bonds provide a way for the corporation to issue debt in the form of bonds and later convert it to equity at a price per share that is more than the current per share price of the stock in the open equity market.[21] This feature is attractive because it allows the corporation to "sell" stock at a higher future price. In other words, if you convert your bonds to stock, then the company is off the hook in terms of repaying the initial loan you made to them when you bought the bond.

EQUITY MARKETS

The table below shows the distribution of stock ownership of equity securities in the United States. Households dominate, owning over 40% of outstanding corporate equities. Pension funds, both private and public, are the largest institutional holders of stock, followed by mutual funds and foreign investors. These investors come to own equity securities through either primary or secondary market transactions.

---

[21] **Equity market** is a fancy way to say stock market.

Households Dominate The Holdings of Equity Securities		
Holder	**Amount**	**Relative Amount**
Households	$5,349,000,000	41.9%
Pension Funds	$3,059,000,000	24.0%
Mutual Funds	$2,029,000,000	15.9%
Foreign Investors	$934,000,000	7.3%
Insurance Companies	$765,000,000	6.0%
Bank Personal Trusts	$433,000,000	3.4%
Other	$189,000,000	1.5%
Total	**$12,758, 000,000**	100.0%

Source: Federal Reserve, Flow of Funds Account of the United States, Third Quarter 1998.

Primary Market

New issues of securities are called primary offerings. Stock purchases through primary offerings are called **primary market** transactions. The company can use the funds raised by the sale of securities in primary offerings to expand production, enter new markets, further research and enhance other aspects of the firm's operations.[22]

If the company has never before offered a particular type of security to the public, meaning the security is not currently trading in the secondary market, the primary offering is called an **unseasoned offering**—also called an **initial public offering (IPO)**. If the firm has already issued similar equity

---

[22] For this book **firm, company** and **corporation** mean the same thing, and I use these words interchangeably.

securities (stocks) that are trading in the secondary market, and is offering more of the same class of stock, this is known as a **seasoned offering**.

Here is what I mean. Wal-Mart (WMT) "went public" in 1978, making its first IPO of common stock that immediately started trading on the New York Stock Exchange under the ticker symbol "WMT." This was an unseasoned offering, because it had never issued public shares before. Once the stock has traded on the exchange, it is said to have "seasoned" like an aged wine. When WMT issued more shares of the same common stock, it was called a seasoned offering because it was more of the same stock being pumped onto the market.

A **ticker symbol**, also simply called a **symbol**, is a system of letters used to uniquely identify a stock or mutual fund. Symbols with up to three letters are used for stocks which are listed and trade on the NYSE. Symbols with four letters are used for NASDAQ stocks. Symbols with five letters are used for NASDAQ stocks that are not single issues of common stock. Symbols with five letters ending in X are used for mutual funds.

Companies raise money when they can sell seasoned offerings to the public. They don't have to pay principal and interest to bondholders or loan payments to banks when they capitalize (raise money) through seasoned offerings. A seasoned offering is what a company does to raise more money for operations.

All securities undergo a single primary offering of an IPO in which the issuer receives the proceeds of the offering and the investors receive equity securities. Thereafter, whenever the securities are bought or sold, the transaction occurs in the secondary market and money and shares are transferred between shareholders as they buy and sell the stock among themselves.

New issues of equity securities may be sold directly to investors by the issuing corporation, but are usually distributed by an **investment banker** in an underwritten offering, a private placement or a shelf registration. The most common distribution method is an **underwritten offering** in which the investment banker purchases the securities from the firm at a guaranteed amount known as the **net proceeds,** then resells the equity securities to public investors for a greater amount, called the **gross proceeds**. The difference between the net and the gross proceeds is called the **underwriter's spread,** which compensates the investment banker for the expenses and risks involved in the offering.

Also, some equity securities are distributed through **private placements** in which the investment banker acts only as the company's agent and receives a commission for placing equity securities with accredited and qualified investors— individuals of high net worth and income.

In addition, occasionally a company will place equity securities with its existing shareholders through a rights offering. In a **rights offering,** a company's existing stockholders are given the rights to purchase additional shares at a slightly below-market price in proportion to the current ownership in the company. Stockholders can exercise their rights to own the equity security offered or sell off their rights to another investor. The best description of the highly profitable use of rights offerings is eloquently described by the financial journalist Nicolas Darvas in his true story "How I Made $2,000,000 in the Stock Market." This highly recommended book is available on Amazon.

An important innovation in the sale of new corporate securities (equity and debt) is shelf registration. **Shelf registration** permits a corporation to register a quantity of securities with the

Fact: In 2000, CEO Steven Jobs' crony-controlled board of directors at Apple Computer (AAPL) awarded him 20 million shares in employee stock options. By 2006, those shares were worth over $500,000,000!

Securities and Exchange Commission (SEC) and sell them over time rather than all at once, thus the issuer is able to save time and money through a single registration. In addition, with shelf registration, securities can be brought to market with little notice—thereby providing the issuer with maximum flexibility in timing a seasoned offering to take advantage of favorable market conditions. For example, **Sirius Satellite Radio (SIRI)** filed a $500 million shelf registration on July 5th, 2001 when the stock price was around $10 per share. This shelf registration allows them to raise money cheaply and quickly because they don't have to hassle with the SEC. They can issue a seasoned offering very quickly due to the shelf registration.

Factors Affecting Underwriter Spreads

The **gross proceeds** of an underwritten offering, you'll recall, is the total profit of selling the stock. The **net proceeds** are what is left over after the investment banker takes his commissions and fees for helping the corporation make the offering. In an underwritten offering, the investment banker's profit, the **underwriter's spread**, is the difference between the gross proceeds and the net proceeds. Several factors affect the size of the spread.

First, the underwriter's spread is inversely related to the size of the offering. In other words, the larger the offering, the smaller the spread tends to be as a percentage of the amount of funds being raised by the company. Second, the more uncertain the investment bankers are concerning the market price of the equity securities being offered the larger the under-writer's spread tends to be. The reason for this is that in an underwritten offering, especially an unseasoned offering, the investment banker bears all of the price risk—the investment banker could lose money if the price of the stock turns out to be lower than anticipated because the public doesn't want it. Third, shelf registrations tend to have lower spreads than ordinary offerings. This is due in part to the fact that larger, more well-known companies employ shelf registrations. The stock is already trading so there is less price risk to the underwriter.

Secondary Markets

Any trade of a security after its primary offering is called a **secondary market transaction**. When an investor buys 100 shares of IBM on the New York Stock Exchange, the proceeds of the sale do not go to IBM, but rather to the investor who sold the shares. In the United States, most secondary market

Nader Tavakoli, CEO of Ambac stares in disbelief at Jim Millstein, lead bond restructuring adviser for the commonwealth government as Lisa Donahue hosts a heated discussion of Puerto Rico insolvency.

equity trading is done either on organized exchanges, such as the New York Stock Exchange (NYSE), or in the **over-the-counter market (OTC)**.

From an investor's perspective, the function of secondary markets is to provide liquidity at fair prices. **Liquidity** is the speed at which an asset such as stock, bonds, or real estate can be converted into cash without a discount. Stocks and bonds, for instance are much more liquid than real estate. The degree of liquidity dictates how fast you can get in and out of the market at what you feel is a good price. An **asset** is any item of economic value owned by an individual or corporation, especially that which could be converted to cash.[23]

Investors want liquidity in the stock market for three reasons. *First*, they have new information about a particular stock of a company and want to buy or sell. *Second*, they want to save by setting aside money for retirement or a rainy day by buying securities or they need money now and un-save by selling securities. *Third*, their attitude towards risk changes and they wish to restructure the composition of their portfolio.

Liquidity exists if investors can trade large amounts of securities without affecting prices—a high volume of trading does not make the price bounce around much. Prices are said to be fair if they reflect the underlying value of the security correctly.

---

[23] Examples are cash, securities, accounts receivable, inventory, office equipment, real estate, a car, and other property. On a balance sheet, assets are equal to the sum of liabilities, common stock, preferred stock, and retained earnings. From an accounting perspective, assets are divided into the following categories: current assets (cash and other liquid items), long-term assets (real estate, plant, equipment), prepaid and deferred assets (expenditures for future costs such as insurance, rent, interest), and intangible assets (trademarks, patents, copyrights, goodwill).

There are three liquidity-related characteristics of a secondary market that investors find desirable: depth, breadth, and resiliency. *First,* a secondary market is said to have **depth** if there are orders both above and below the level at which the security is currently trading—people are waiting on the sidelines at each increment to enter the market if the price goes up or down. When a security trades in a deep market, temporary imbalances of purchase or sale orders (that would otherwise create substantial price changes) encounter offsetting, and hence stabilizing, sale or purchase orders reducing noisy price volatility. *Second,* a secondary market is said to have **breadth** if orders in large volume give its market depth—lots of people are waiting to enter the market at each price increment above and below the current trading price. The broader the market for a stock, the greater the potential for stabilization of temporary price changes that may arise from order imbalances. *Third,* a market is **resilient** if new orders pour in promptly in response to price changes that result from temporary order imbalances—investors act very quickly buying or selling when the stock price moves up or down. For a market to be resilient, investors must be able to quickly learn when stock price changes occur. However, what investors are most concerned with is having complete information concerning a security's current price and where that price can be obtained.

There are four kinds of secondary market: direct search, brokered, dealer and auction. Each of these types of secondary markets differs according to the amount of information you get concerning prices. You need to know the nuances of these different markets as a stock investor.

Direct Search Secondary Markets

The secondary market that offers you the *least* complete price information—buyers and sellers have to search for one another directly – is the **direct search secondary market**. Because the full cost of locating and bargaining with a willing and capable trading partner is paid for by an individual investor, there is only a small incentive to conduct a thorough search among all possible trading partners in the market for the best possible price. Not searching because of high cost means that, at the time a trade is agreed upon by the two investors, at least one of the participants could have gotten a better price if they were in contact with some participant they never found. Stocks that trade in direct search markets are ones that people buy and sell very infrequently. This means a third party, like a broker or a dealer, has no profit incentive to provide any kind of service to facilitate trading in direct search markets.

The common stock of small companies, especially small banks, trade in direct search markets. Buyers and sellers of those issues must rely on word-of-mouth communication to attract compatible trading partners to buy from or sell to. Very few trades means there is no economical way of broadcasting quotations or transaction prices, trades can occur at the same time at quite different prices, and transactions frequently occur away from the best possible price. My advice to you is to stay away from stocks that you have to buy and sell by direct search.

Brokered Secondary Markets

When trading in an issue (a specific stock) becomes sufficiently heavy, brokers begin to offer specialized search services to market participants. For a fee, called a **brokerage commission**, brokers help find compatible trading partners and negotiate acceptable transaction prices for their clients.

Brokers are more likely to be involved in the market when there are economies of scale in searching—when they can make money because a lot of investors are in the market. If brokers can fill two customers' orders at less than twice the cost of the direct search—that would otherwise be conducted by each of those customers— then brokers will offer their services. By charging a commission less than the cost of

Tip: Online discount stock brokerages allow you to buy and sell in the convenience of your home at low cost with no human intervention. Examples: TDAmeritrade. com, E-trade.com, ScottTrade. com, and fidelity.com.

direct search, they give investors an incentive to make use of the broker's special information. This is important because they can profitably acquire the business of both investors by charging a commission somewhat less than the cost of a direct search.

Since brokers are frequently in contact with many market participants on a continuing basis, they are likely to know what a "fair" price is for a transaction. Brokers will usually know whether the offering price of a seller can easily be improved upon by looking elsewhere. They know whether it is closest to the lowest offer price likely to be offered by some other investor in the market. Brokers provide these trade matching services at a cheaper price than the investor's own cost of searching. Stock and bond brokers also arrange transactions closer to the best available price for the investor than is possible in a direct search market. Their extensive contacts provide them with a pool of price information that individual investors could not economically duplicate because it is too costly.

Dealer Secondary Markets

A brokered market is better than direct search, but has the disadvantage that it can't guarantee the investor's orders will be executed promptly. Uncertainty about the speed of execution creates price risk. While a broker is searching out a willing and able trading partner for a client, securities prices may change and the client may suffer a loss. However, if trading in a stock issue is active enough, some market participants may begin to maintain bid and offer quotations of their own. **Dealers** buy and sell their own inventory at their own quoted prices. Dealer secondary markets eliminate the need for time-consuming searches for trading partners because investors know they can buy or sell immediately at quotes given by a dealer.

Dealers earn a living (in part) by selling stocks at an asking price greater than the bid price they pay. Their **bid-ask spread** compensates them for providing liquidity of an immediately available market to occasional market participants—you buy and sell every now and then but they are there ready every day to help, for a price. The bid-ask spread also pays for the risk dealers incur when they position an issue in their inventory—the dealer may lose money on the stock he or she is holding in inventory to sell to you or buy from you when you come around every so often.

The bid-ask spread is really just two prices people are willing to pay or accept for their stock. The **bid price** is the highest price that someone is willing to pay to buy your shares of stock; this also means it is the highest price you can expect to get for your shares of stock when selling. It is always lower than the ask price. The **ask price** is the lowest price you can pay for a stock; this is because it's the lowest price any seller is offering their shares of stock for. Although the ask price might be $14, you might pay slightly higher if you put in a large order, because the dealer must poke around to find other sellers to fill the order.

In most cases, dealers do not quote identical prices for a stock because they disagree about the value or because they have different inventory objectives—they may want to get rid of the stock they have or they are loading up. Even in a dealer market, investors have to search out the best prices for their trades. The expense of contacting several dealers to obtain comparative quotations is borne by investors. But since dealers have an incentive to advertise, their willingness to buy and sell their inventory will be well known and such contracts can usually be completed quickly. The ease of searching among dealers guarantees that those dealers quoting the best price will be most likely to do business with investors.

Dealer markets provide investors with the opportunity for an immediate execution of their orders. And, although dealer markets can usually be searched more rapidly and cheaply than a direct search or brokered markets, they do have several disadvantages. No one can guarantee that the quotation of a particular dealer could be improved upon by contacting another dealer. This being the case, investors operating in dealer markets have to bear some cost of searching for the best price.

A second factor in dealer trading is the expense of a dealer's bid-ask spread. Suppose one investor is willing to sell a stock at $99, and another is willing to buy the same stock at $101. If they could meet, they would agree to trade at $100, each doing better than the dealer's reservation price. Rather than incur the expense of searching each other out, however, they might both prefer to trade with a dealer bidding on the stock at $99½ and offering the stock at $100½. They would be giving up a half point each to the dealer's bid-ask spread to avoid the cost of the search, even though they could have done better if each investor had known the other was seeking to trade. Although dealers stand ready to trade, it would be better for the investors if they could trade directly, inside the dealer's quotations, whenever possible.

Auction Secondary Markets

Auction markets provide centralized procedures for the exposure of purchase and sale orders to all market participants simultaneously. In other words, an auction market is a place everyone who wants to buy and sell can go. This is important because auction markets virtually eliminate the expense of locating compatible partners and bargaining for a favorable price. The communication of price information in an auction market may be oral, if all participants are physically located in the same place, or the information can be transmitted electronically.

Dr. Bill Garner M.D. discusses pharma startup opportunities in Puerto Rico as Dr. Mark Schwartz listens on.

Factors Affecting the Size of Bid Ask Spreads

Spreads between dealers' bid and ask prices are not the same for all equity securities. They range from as low as a fraction of a cent on frequently traded issues to several dollars on securities that hardly ever trade. The wide range of spread sizes exist because of differences in the trading costs of various securities. These trading costs are a function of issue characteristics of the stock and its trading patterns. The factors affecting the size of the bid-ask spread for equity securities include the stock price, recent transaction size, transaction frequency, and the presence in the market of investors trading on inside information.

Other things being the same, the bid-ask spread for a stock should be proportional to its price. That is, higher priced stocks tend to have larger absolute spreads. However, due to some fixed transactions costs, higher priced stocks tend to have lower bid-ask spreads in percentage terms.

Extremely small transactions and extremely large transactions tend to have larger bid ask spreads in percentage terms, because they are challenging for the broker to fill. Small transactions generate larger spreads because of the hassle of filling small orders in less than a **round lot** of 100 shares. For larger transactions, the spread between bid and ask prices is larger because the dealer is providing more of a liquidity service than would be the case for a normal-size trade—large orders require a lot of smaller buyers that the broker has to find.

The frequency of trades for a particular stock also impacts the bid-ask spread. Since the dealer is providing liquidity service, the more frequently a stock is traded, the less costly it is for the dealer to provide investors with liquidity so that their orders clear. In other words, if there are a lot of people who are buying and selling the stock right now, it is a lot easier for the dealer to find buyers and sellers. This is because the dealer can hold a smaller inventory of the stock when trading is more frequent, decreasing inventory costs.

The presence of **short-term insiders**, traders who have short-term inside information the public doesn't about the short-term value of a stock, will cause dealers to widen the bid-ask spread. This is important to understand because dealers may lose in transactions with better-informed traders in the short run. Traders who have **short-term inside information** will sell when the current price is too high because they know the price will quickly drop. An example of short-term inside information would be a corporate secretary secretly photocopying a confidential report about an upcoming merger and then giving it to her husband. In this case, the couple would know that the stock price would go up or down the day the news of the merger is released.

Dealers who transact with such traders end up paying a price that is too high when the short-term inside information is bad news about the stock. Alternatively, dealers will end up selling at too low of a price when the short-term inside information is favorable and short-term insiders know that the stock is going to rise. Unfortunately, dealers find it difficult to separate traders acting on short-term inside information from those traders without such information. Traders and investors without short-term inside information are known as **uninformed**. Dealers increase the spread to compensate for potential losses when they know that they are probably trading against investors with short-term inside information.

EQUITY TRADING

Several thousand stocks are listed and trade on organized stock exchanges, while there exist perhaps 30,000 other "unlisted" stock issues that the public can buy and sell but are not listed on any exchange. These "unlisted" stocks trade in the over-the-counter market, also called the **OTC** market.

Over-The-Counter and NASDAQ

Securities not sold on an organized exchange like the NYSE are said to be traded **over-the-counter (OTC)**. A stock may not be listed on an organized exchange for several reasons, including lack of widespread investor interest, small issue size, or insufficient order flow. The OTC stock market is a dealer market. Since different OTC issues are not usually close substitutes for each other, a dealer with limited capital can make a successful market, even in a relatively narrow range of stocks, by carrying inventory of the stock. **Inventory** here is defined as securities, in this case stocks, bought and held by a broker or dealer for resale. Thus, there are many relatively small **OTC dealers**. OTC dealers, however, often concentrate their trading in particular industry groups or geographical areas, like the high-tech industry or companies located in California. At least 30,000 various types of equity securities are traded in the OTC market. However, only about 15,000 of these securities are actively traded.

When a customer places an order to buy or sell a stock in the OTC market, the broker or dealer contacts other dealers who have that particular stock for sale. Public orders for purchase or sale of stock are often executed by brokers acting as agents for their own customers. When handling a public order, a broker will contact several dealers to search out the best price.

Tip: Get started today setting aside whatever you can for investing. Many stock market millionaires started setting aside as little as $5 or $10 per week for the stock market. They sent it in monthly or let it build up and contributed every three to six months or so. Identifying a good stock and buying every chance you can is called **dollar-cost averaging**. *If you don't start somewhere, you will never get anywhere!*

When a broker is satisfied with a dealer's quoted price, he or she will complete the buying or selling transaction with that dealer and charge his or her customer the same price, plus a commission for the brokerage services. Investors use brokers to locate the most favorable dealer because investors are usually unfamiliar with which dealers are making markets in specific stocks. Investors also use brokers because they can contact dealers at a lower cost. Brokers can capitalize on economies of scale in searching; it costs the broker a lot less money to search for an offsetting buyer or seller of stock than the investor.

When handling a customer's order, a broker has two problems to deal with. First, he has to figure out which dealers are market makers in the stock the investor is buying or selling. Second, he must figure out which of these dealers is quoting the best price to you. Before 1971, the first problem was easily resolved by looking at the **"pink sheets"** compiled by the **National Quotation Bureau (NQB)**. These sheets, printed on pink paper, were distributed daily to subscribing dealers starting in 1919. The pink sheets listed bid and ask prices submitted by dealers to NQB the previous afternoon. The NQB runs the over-the-counter market.

Because of the print delay, pink sheet quotes were always "stale." Nearly a day passed between the submission of a quote to NQB and the distribution of the pink sheets to market participants, including your broker. More generally, a dealer could not be expected to sell a stock on Thursday morning at the offer price quoted Wednesday afternoon. Thus, the pink sheets are more a vehicle for advertising interest in an issue than for publishing firm price quotations. The pink sheets are of real value, however, for figuring out which dealers are active in a given issue.

After a broker has found out which firms are dealing in a stock, he or she must next locate the best price for you. Up to 1971, this search process was conducted exclusively by telephone or Teletype. A broker handling an order typically called several dealers, got hit with big telephone charges and wasted a lot of his or her time calling around. These costs reduced the desire of the broker to make a complete search of the OTC dealer market and often resulted in orders filled at bad prices—these are executions away from better (undiscovered) prices.

A major development of the OTC market occurred in 1971, when the **National Association of Securities Dealers (NASD)** introduced an automatic computer-based quotation system (**NASDAQ**). The system offers continuous bid and ask prices for most actively traded OTC stocks. NASDAQ is basically an electronic pink sheet that significantly helped the existing structure of the OTC market. NASDAQ accelerated the disclosure of price information and fundamentally altered the structure of the OTC market.

There are three levels of access to the NASDAQ system. **Level 3 NASDAQ terminals** are available only to dealers and allow them to enter bid and ask quotations for specific stocks directly into the system. These quotations, together with information identifying the stock and the dealer, appear within seconds on the terminals of other dealers and brokers. For this reason, the NASDAQ never has stale prices like the pink sheets. **Level 2 NASDAQ terminals** display all dealer price bid and ask quotations for a given stock, but do not allow quotations to be changed on the terminal. These terminals are available to brokers and institutions. **Level 1 NASDAQ terminals** provide only the best bid and ask prices (called the **inside quote**) for a stock. These terminals are used by stockbrokers when quoting prices to their customers.

NASDAQ's most important contribution to enhancing the OTC market was accelerating the disclosure of dealer quotations to brokers. NASDAQ did little to increase the identification of dealers beyond the reach of the pink sheets, but it did greatly increase the efficiency of a broker's search for the best bid and ask prices. NASDAQ greatly reduced the amount of trading away from the best available prices. Whereas investors were overpaying for stock they bought or underselling the stock they sold, with NASDAQ, more transactions were taking place at true market value.

Stock Exchanges

A stock exchange is actually two markets in one. First, it is a place where a new company can raise millions or billions of dollars overnight by offering ownership to hundreds or thousands of small investors. These pieces of ownership, as I mentioned before, are called "shares of stock." Secondly, the exchange is a place where people can sell their stock to someone else whenever they wish.

You can be in the airline business one day and then get out of it in the next and into the automobile industry. This ability to get in and out and get paid for your investment drives the success of stock exchanges worldwide. Forty percent of American families own stock in U.S. companies, either directly or through mutual funds and pension plans. The exchange lets these families know how they are doing financially by placing a value on their stock.

The **New York Stock Exchange (NYSE)**, the pre-eminent, largest and most organized stock exchange in the United States, is an example of an auction market. Other **regional stock exchanges** in the United States include the **American Stock Exchange (AMEX)** in New York, the Pacific Stock Exchange in both San Francisco and Los Angeles, the Chicago Stock Exchange (formerly the Midwest Stock Exchange), the Philadelphia Stock Exchange, the Boston Stock Exchange, and the Cincinnati Stock Exchange. The table below shows the trading volume on the major United States exchanges. The NASDAQ and the NYSE account for the clear majority of stock trading while regional exchanges account for little trading volume in the United States.

United States Trading Volume	
Exchange	**Trading Volume (millions of shares)**
NASDAQ	858.70
NYSE	737.14
AMEX	32.28

Source: The Wall Street Journal, February 26, 1999.

All transactions completed in a stock listed on the NYSE occur at a unique place on the floor of the exchange, called a **post**. There are three major sources of active bid prices and ask prices in a stock issue available at a post: (1) **floor brokers** executing customer stock orders, (2) **limit orders** for stock left with the specialist for execution and, (3) **specialists** in the stock buying and selling for his or her own account. Since trading is physically localized, the best available bid-and-offer quotes are very available. Competition and ease of communication among market participants gathered at a post ensure there is the right priority of execution and also fill bids above the lowest ask price or asks below the highest bid price for the stock.

Orders from the public are transmitted by Internet, telephone or telex from brokerage houses to brokers on the floor of the NYSE, who bring the orders to the appropriate posts for execution. Most of these orders are either market orders or limit orders.

A **market order** is an order to buy or sell at the best possible price available at the time the order reaches the post. The broker carrying a market order to a post might execute the order immediately, or might hold back all or part of the order for a short time to see if a better price is available. He or she may also decide to quote a price on the transaction that is inside the current bid-and-ask prices. This gets the client's order in front of other orders at the post and reduces the amount of time the broker will have to wait until completing the trade.

A **limit order** is an order to buy or sell at a designated price, or better if possible. The designated price that the client requests is called the **limit price.** Investors place limit orders when they want to buy or sell at a price somewhere above or somewhere below the bid-ask spread. In other words, a limit order is a desired bid for stock when buying or asking price when selling a stock. A floor broker handling a limit order to buy at or below a stated price, or to sell at or above a stated price, will usually stand by the post with his order if the limit price on the order is near the current market price, which is, of course, the current bid and ask prices.

When a limit order is at a price that is not very close to the current market prices (the bid and ask), the broker handling the order knows it is not likely that the order will be executed anytime soon. For example, a **buy limit order** at $50 on a stock currently trading at $55 may not be satisfied for days, and may never be satisfied. The broker presenting the order wants to make sure that the order is executed as soon as possible, but does not want to stand around tendering the order to the post forever. As an alternative to maintaining a physical presence at the post (tendering the order to the post), the broker can enter the limit order on the order book maintained by the specialist. Orders on the book are treated with other orders in terms of price priority. No trades can take place at a price unless all bids above and all asks below that level have been cleared from the book. In other words, the market has to move up through all of the sell limit orders in the book to hit your **sell limit order**. Alternatively, the market has to move down through all other buy limit orders in the book between your buy limit order price at the bottom of the inside spread before it is filled. Entering a limit order on a specialist's book gives a great alternative to floor brokers who would otherwise have to maintain a physical presence at a post to keep a limit buy or limit sell order active.

Specialists provide the third source of bids and asks in listed securities. On the NYSE, specialists are members of the exchange who are both dealers and order clerks. Specialists have to maintain both bid and ask price quotations at all times, good for at least one round lot of the issue in which they specialize. In this respect specialists act as dealers, trading for their own account and at their own risk. NYSE specialists also maintain the book of limit orders left by floor brokers, and in this way they act as order clerks.

Trap: Most people who fail do so because they never start — they dream and never act. North American football legend **Fran Tarkington** held the quarterback record of 3,674 pass completions until 1995. The rest of the story is that he also held the record for number of passing failures — he simply threw more passes than anyone else! After retiring from football, he became a motivational speaker, teaching people the importance of acting toward what they want out of life.

Stocks that are heavily traded do not need specialists—specialist activities in these stocks have been criticized as opportunistic by people off the exchange. Trading on the floor of the NYSE in stocks that have sufficiently heavy trading volume ensures that there is always an active bid or ask available from either floor brokers or the limit order book. For heavily traded stocks, the specialist's dealer function of liquidity to get your orders filled really fast is not a big deal—a lot of people buying and selling a stock in itself creates liquidity. In many stocks, public trading interest is not as strong—it is sporadic—infrequent. In these cases, the obligation of the specialist to provide liquidity service of immediate execution is important. In fact, if the prices of the best purchase and sell orders on the specialist's book have a wide spread (which is common for infrequently traded stocks), the specialist may be the sole source of an economical market for immediate transaction because there is nobody to buy the stock you are selling or sell you the stock you want to buy.

Global Stock Markets

The secondary markets for equity securities are very competitive. Better communications and computer technology have reduced transaction costs, making it easier for other financial intermediaries to compete with securities firms.

This has kicked up heated competition among national exchanges, regional exchanges, over-the-counter markets and foreign exchanges. The trend of change of the exchanges is related to forces of technology and competition—the emergence of a national market system, online discount trading, the move toward 24-hour trading of equity securities, and globalization of equity markets are making investing more interconnected.

This has flattened the investment world. A well-trained diligent stock investor has the same quality of information as a Wall Street hedge fund manager.

The Securities Act Amendment of 1975 mandated that the Securities and Exchange Commission (SEC), the primary regulator of U.S. financial markets, move toward creating a national market. In its ideal form, a national market system would have a huge computer system recording and reporting transactions, regardless of location. It would also be a system that allows investors to get price information from any exchange instantaneously, and to buy or sell stock at the best price regardless of location. Progress has been made toward electronically linking the national exchanges, regional exchanges and over-the-counter markets, but we are still many years away from a truly nationwide system.

There is competitive pressure to link international stock markets as well. Many U.S. firms are issuing stocks on overseas exchanges to take advantage of differences in tax laws, to increase their visibility and reputation worldwide, and to avoid driving down the share price by flooding a local stock market. In 1986, the London Stock Exchange created a computer network similar to the NASDAQ system that permitted U.S. and Japanese investment firms to enter trades on the British system. This development was important because it

CEO Dave Watkin's comments are the focus of discussion of tech startups in Puerto Rico.

created a virtual 24-hour global trading environment, given time differences between New York, London and Tokyo. For this reason, many U.S. companies are now listed on exchanges in all three locations. This has increased interest in Europe for trading stocks of U.S. companies by European investors.

Stock exchanges in the United States are panicked about losing business to overseas stock markets. As a step toward increasing the global competitiveness of the U.S. financial markets, the SEC permits after-hours on the NYSE. Previously, trading on the NYSE took place between 9:30am and 4:00pm Eastern time. The NYSE now has several after-hours sessions during which shares trade electronically after the close until mid-evening and before the open starting mid-morning. The biggest beneficiaries of the NYSE's move toward globalization will be U.S. companies that expect to broaden the market for their securities. The flow of capital across international boundaries makes it easier for firms to raise money for overseas operations.

American Depository Receipts

Japan's Sony and Switzerland's Nestlé are two among many foreign corporations that have discovered the benefits of trading their stock in the United States. Unfamiliar market practices, confusing tax legislation, incomplete shareholder communications, and a total lack of effective avenues for legal recourse tend to discourage U.S. investors from buying shares in foreign stock markets. On the other hand, the disclosure and reporting requirements of the SEC for foreign compliance have kept all but the largest overseas firms from directly listing their shares of stock on the New York Stock Exchange as an American Depository Receipt (ADR).

Many foreign companies overcome these road blocks and tap into the U.S. market by means of **American Depository Receipts (ADR)**. **ADRs** are dollar-denominated claims issued by U.S. banks representing the ownership of shares of a foreign stock held on deposit in a U.S. bank for U.S. investors. ADRs are sponsored or unsponsored.

Trap: Because of low interest rates, many fixed income investors look for higher yielding, lower-quality "junk" bonds. Wall Street tries to make these double digit returns in the junk-bond market seem secure to suck investors in. Double digit yielding **Junk bonds** carry enormous risk. In fact, they are a form of fixed income gambling. Many of these issues go into default, becoming worthless. Without realizing it, these investors are purchasing sub-standard securities in the hope that nothing goes wrong.

A **sponsored ADR** is one for which the issuing (foreign) company absorbs the legal and financial costs of creating and trading the security. An unsponsored ADR is one in which the issuing firm is not involved with the issue at all or may even oppose it. **Unsponsored ADRs** typically result from U.S. investor demand for shares of a particular foreign company. With over 1,600 ADRs from 63 countries trading in the United States, they are very popular with U.S. investors, at least in part because they allow U.S. investors to diversify internationally. However, the ownership claim is covered by American securities laws stipulating that dividends must be paid in American dollars (dividends on the underlying shares are converted from foreign currency into U.S. dollars and then paid to U.S. investors). In other words, you avoid exchange rate risk when you buy ADRs.

Each ADR can represent a fraction or a multiple of a share of the foreign company. This means that the price of the ADR is within the range of share prices for comparable companies traded in the United States. Because an ADR can be converted into ownership of underlying shares, arbitrage ensures a reasonable price on this claim against foreign-currency-denominated stock. **Arbitrage** is the purchase of stock in one market for immediate resale in another in order to profit from a price discrepancy. Arbitrage is important because it keeps prices in line—IBM stock sells for the same price on the NYSE as it does on the AMEX as it does in London because of arbitrage.

For example, Gerdua S.A ("GGB") established an American Depository Receipt program on the New York Stock Exchange on March 10, 1999. Gerdua is one of Brazil's leading steel producers. Other foreign companies that have ADRs include Unilever, Royal Dutch Shell, British Airways, Toyota, Bayer, Gucci, De Beers and Siemens. JP Morgan, a large U.S. investment bank and the leading sponsor of ADRs, has established a web site (ADR.com) devoted to providing information on ADRs.

REGULATION OF EQUITY MARKETS

Trading in securities in the United States is regulated by several laws. The two most important laws are the **Securities Act of 1933** and the **Securities Exchange Act of 1934**. The 1933 act requires full disclosure of relevant information relating to the issue of new stock in the primary market. This is the act that requires full registration of an IPO and the issuance of a prospectus that details the recent financial history of the company. SEC acceptance of a prospectus or financial report does not mean that it views the security as a good investment! The SEC is only concerned that the relevant facts are disclosed to investors—you have to make your own evaluation of the stock's value. The 1934 act established the **Securities and Exchange Commission (SEC)** to administer the provisions of the 1933 act. It also extended the disclosure of the 1933 act by requiring firms with outstanding stocks—seasoned equities—on secondary exchanges to disclose relevant financial information periodically.

The 1934 act also allowed the SEC to register and regulate securities exchanges, over-the-counter (OTC) trading, brokers and dealers. The 1934 act established the SEC as the administrative agency responsible for broad oversight of all U.S. secondary markets. In addition to federal regulations, security trading is subject to state laws. The laws providing for state regulation of securities activities are generally known as **"blue sky" laws** because they prevent the false promotion of securities by fraudsters backed by nothing more than blue sky.

EQUITY VALUATION BASICS

The most used valuation metric is market cap.

Market capitalization is the total value of all outstanding shares of a company. To calculate market capitalization, simply multiply the total number of shares outstanding—of each class of common and preferred stock that the company has trading in the market—times its corresponding share price. Assume, for instance, that a company has 1,000,000 shares of common stock outstanding trading at $15 per share and 2,000,000 shares of preferred stock trading at $10 per share. The market capitalization of the company is:

$$Market\ Cap = (1,000,000\ Shares)\left(\frac{\$15}{Share}\right) + (2,000,000\ Shares)\left(\frac{\$10}{Share}\right) = \$35,000,000$$

Book value is the value of the company as shown on the firm's balance sheet. This is the value of everything the company owns, less everything it owes. This is very simple in concept, but very difficult to actually calculate. There are many areas of accounting standards promoted by the **Financial Accounting Standards Board (FASB)** where wide latitude in interpretation makes it possible for the balance sheet to not necessarily reflect the true value of the firm. It may actually be impossible to tell what the firm is really worth, because inside corporate executives have generated financial statements to reflect their own agenda. This agenda may have nothing to do with informing the public as to the true accounting value of the firm. I have not yet found book value to be a useful filter to spot stocks that can beat the market.

Fundamental analysis focuses on the company's financial information and uses not only the company balance sheet, but also the income and cash flow statements. The primary concept here is that implied earnings (cash flow) increases the value of the firm. Since the shareholders are the owners of the firm, the idea is that bottom-line profits increase the share price of the company's stock.

Technical analysis attempts to predict the future direction of stock price movements based on two major types of information: (1) price and volume behavior and (2) investor sentiment. Technical analysis techniques are centuries old and enormous in number.

STOCK MARKET INDEXES

Stock market indexes provide a useful tool to summarize the vast array of information generated by the continuous buying and selling of stocks. At the same time, the use of market indexes presents two problems. First, many different indexes compete for our attention. Second, indexes differ in their composition and can give contradictory information regarding aggregate price movements in the stock market.

When constructing a stock market index, the base index value and the starting date have to be selected. The choice is completely arbitrary, since absolute index values are meaningless. Only the relative changes give you useful information. For example, knowing only that a particular stock market index finished the year at a level of 354.7 is of no value to you. However, if you also know that the same index finished the previous year at a level of

Fact: It is vital to your success as an investor that you select analysis techniques that are harmonious with your personality!

331.5, then you can calculate that the stock market—as measured by this particular index—rose approximately 7% over the past year.

The next decision is which stocks should be included in the index. There are three methods for deciding stock index composition: *(1) the index can represent a stock exchange and include all the stocks traded on the exchange, (2) the organization producing the index can subjectively select the stocks to be included, or (3) the stocks to be included can be selected based on some objective measure such as market value, which is simply the number of shares outstanding times the price per share.* Often, the stocks in an index are divided into groups so that the index represents the performance of various industry segments such as industrial, transportation or utility companies. Regardless of the method chosen for selecting the stocks, the composition of an index can change whenever companies merge or are de-listed from an exchange.

Once the firms to be included in an index are selected, the stocks must be combined in certain proportions to construct the index. Each stock, therefore, must be assigned some relative weight. One of two approaches typically is used to assign relative weights when calculating stock market indexes: (1) by the price of the company's stock or (2) by the market value of the company, market value meaning the same thing as market capitalization.

Price-Weighted Indexes

A **price-weighted index** is first computed by summing the prices of the individual stocks composing the index. The sum of the prices is then divided by a "divisor" to yield the chosen base index value. Thereafter, as stock prices change, the divisor remains constant unless there is an event like a stock split,[24] a stock dividend,[25] or a change in index composition. If such a situation arises, then the divisor is adjusted so that the index value is not affected by the event in question.

For example, if the price per share of stocks A, B, and C in a price-weighted index were $20, $10, and $50 respectively, then the prices would sum to $80. If the base index value is to be 100, then the initial divisor would be 0.8 ... $100 = \dfrac{80}{0.8}$. On the next trading day, say prices per share of the stocks change to $25, $10, and $40. Now the new sum of share prices would be $75 and the price weighted index value would be $\dfrac{75}{0.8}$ = 93.75, or 6.25% lower.

Now assume that stock C undergoes a two-for-one split after the market closes on the second day such that its price per share declines to $20 because $\dfrac{\$40}{2}$ = $20. The sum of the three prices is now $55, but the index should remain the same because the market value of the company did not change. The

---

[24] A stock split is an increase in the number of outstanding shares of a company's stock, such that the proportionate equity of each shareholder remains the same. This requires approval from the board of directors and shareholders. A corporation whose stock is performing well may choose to split its shares, distributing additional shares to existing shareholders. The most common stock split is two-for-one, in which each share becomes two shares. The price per share immediately adjusts to reflect the stock split, since buyers and sellers of the stock all know about the stock split (in this example, the share price would be cut in half). Some companies decide to split if the price rises significantly and is perceived to be too expensive for small investors to afford.

[25] A stock dividend is a dividend paid as additional shares of stock rather than as cash. If dividends paid are in the form of cash, those dividends are taxable. When a company issues a stock dividend, rather than cash, there usually are no tax consequences until the shares are sold.

market value of the company did not change because, even though the price dropped by half, the shares outstanding of the firm doubled. The new divisor is adjusted so that the index stays at 93.75. The new divisor must be $\frac{55}{93.75} = 0.5867$. This remains constant until it must again be adjusted for an event like another split.

Market Value Weighted Indexes

A **market value-weighted index** is computed by calculating the total market value of the firms in the index and the total market value of those firms on the previous trading day. The percentage change in the total market value from one day to the next represents the change in the index. Market-value weighted indexes do not require adjustments for stock splits and stock dividends because they do not affect market capitalization. However, market-value weighted indexes do require adjustment when the composition of the index changes. Market-value weighted indexes are superior because they account for price and firm size at the same time.

Fact: Less than 5% of all U.S. companies give employee stock options to anyone below management! — *The Wall Street Journal*

For example, if stocks A, B, and C described in the example above had outstanding shares of 100 million, 200 million and 10 million, then the total market value for the three stocks on the first day would be $4.5 billion. The total market value on the second day would be $4.9 billion, for an increase of 8.8%. If the market value-weighted index began with a base level of 10 on the first day, then its value on the second day would be 10.88, or 8.8% higher.

If stock C undergoes a two-for-one split after the market closes on the second day so that its price per share declines to $20, then there is no impact on the market value-weighted index. This is because the number of shares outstanding will double to 20 million and company C's market value will remain at $400 million. This means that the total market value of the three stocks in the market value-weighted index continues to be $4.9 billion on the second day and the index will remain at 10.88.

Notice how you arrive at two very different conclusions concerning stock market performance using the price-weighted and market value-weighted indexes in the above examples. Both indexes used the same stocks and the same price changes. However, the price weighted index dropped 6.25% while the market value-weighted index surged 8.8%. This example clearly shows that both the composition of an index and its weighting scheme can have a significant impact on its results. You need to understand how an index is created to understand what it tells you—I personally watch multiple indexes that measure different aspects of the stock market. These are the S&P 500 and DJIA.

Both market value-weighted and price weighted indexes reflect the returns to buy-and-hold investment strategies. If you were to buy each share in an index in proportion to its outstanding market value, the market-value weighted index would perfectly track capital gains on the underlying index (but the return from dividends would not be included). A **capital gain** is another way of saying your profit from buying at a lower price than the price at which you end up selling the stock. Similarly, a price-weighted index tracks the returns on a portfolio composed of equal shares of each company.[26]

The Dow Jones Averages

The most widely cited stock market index is the **Dow Jones Industrial Average (DJIA),** which was first published in 1896. The DJIA is a price-weighted index that originally consisted of 20 stocks with a divisor of 20; this means that the value of the index was simply the average price of the original 20 stocks. In 1928, the DJIA was enlarged to encompass 30 of the largest U.S. industrial stocks and today includes such companies as Verizon, DuPont and Merck. Dow Jones also publishes a price-weighted index of 20 transportation companies, another index composed of 15 utility companies, and a composite index that includes 65 companies making up the industrial, transportation and utility indexes.[27]

Standard and Poor's Indexes

The **Standard and Poor (S&P) 500 Index** is a market-value weighted index that consists of 500 of the largest U.S. stocks drawn from various industries. The stocks included in the S&P 500 track 80% of the market capitalization of all stocks listed on the NYSE, with a few NASDAQ issues thrown in. The base value for the S&P 500 Index was 10 in 1943. The index is computed on a continuous basis during the trading

---

[26] A portfolio is a collection of investments owned by the same individual or organization. These investments often include stocks, which are investments in individual businesses, bonds, which are investments in debt that are designed to earn interest, and mutual funds, which are essentially pools of money from many investors under active management or passively tracking indices.

[27] None of the Dow Jones indexes is adjusted for stock dividends of less than 10 percent.

day. The S&P 500 is divided into two sub-indexes that follow the performance of industrial and utility companies.

The **S&P 400 MidCap Index** is also published by Standard and Poor's. It is market-value weighted and consists of 400 stocks with market values less than those of the stocks in the S&P 500. The S&P 400 MidCap index is useful for following the performance of medium-sized companies.

In addition, Standard and Poor's publishes a market value-weighted small-cap index that tracks 600 companies with market values less than those of the companies in its S&P MidCap 400 index called the **S&P SmallCap 600 index**. The S&P 1500 index includes companies in the S&P 500, the Mid-Cap 400 and the SmallCap 600.

New York Stock Exchange Index

The **New York Stock Exchange composite index**, published since 1966, includes all of the common and preferred stocks listed on the NYSE. In addition to the composite index, the NYSE stocks are divided into four sub-indexes that track the performance of industrial, utility, finance and transportation stocks. All the NYSE indexes are market-value weighted. The base index value for all five indexes was 50 on December 31, 1965.

NASDAQ Indexes

The NASDAQ Composite index, with a base year of 1970, has been compiled continuously since 1971. The index has three categories of companies—industrial, banks, and insurance. It consists of all of the stocks traded through the NASDAQ, including those traded in the **National Market System (NMS)** and those that are not. In 1984, the NASDAQ

National Market System introduced two new indexes, the NASDAQ/NMS Composite Index and the NASDAQ/NMS Industrial Index. Both are weighted by market capitalization and have a base of 100.

Other Stock Indexes

The **American Stock Exchange composite index** includes all common stocks listed on the AMEX; it is a market-value weighted index. The **Russell 3000 stock index** encompasses the largest companies ranked by market capitalization, while the **Russell 1000 stock index** includes the largest 1,000 market capitalization companies. The **Russell 2000 stock index** includes the bottom 2,000 companies in the Russell 3000, so it loosely represents a small-capitalization market index.

A rare smile on the tense bond board discussion of Puerto Rico bankruptcy.

THE STOCK MARKET AS A PREDICTOR OF ECONOMIC ACTIVITY

After every minor and major stock market crash—like **Black Monday** in October of 1987 and the bear decline from 2000 through 2003—there are investors who are terrified that a major recession or even a depression will follow. Ask yourself, *"How realistic are these fears?"* The hard evidence is that the very best time to buy into the stock market is after it has crashed and stock prices are low.

When there are lots of CNN analysts in the popular press foretelling disaster, it can take real guts to buy in, but you must. These fears are based on people's painful memories such as the 1929 stock market crash and the Great Depression that followed. Why do some economists and many investors believe that the stock market can predict economic recessions?

Tip: The best time to buy into the stock market is after a major crash.

First, even if changes in stock prices have no direct effect on the economy, lots of people believing cause recessions. If everyone in the market agrees that a recession is about to happen, investors could, at least in theory, forecast lower corporate profits, bid prices down, and stock prices should drop accordingly. Second, stock price declines reduce the wealth of consumers and could lead to reduced consumption spending leading to lower national income (GNP or GDP). Third, if consumer confidence is adversely affected by stock price declines, consumption spending could decrease.

What really happens?

Empirical evidence by direct research indicates that the stock market is very poor at predicting economic activity. A study by the Federal Reserve Board of Kansas City showed that only 11 of the 27 recessions between 1900 and 1987 were predicted by stock market declines. The answer is, *"Don't worry about it."*

Chapter 4:   The Language of Mutual Funds!

I have a family friend named Sharon who shows all of us how powerful the unconventional wisdom is of *"pay yourself first."* She lived in the same neighborhood where I grew up. There was a big difference in Sharon and her husband Chuck's income and my father and mother's income. Sharon's husband was the local high school principal and she was a beautician. My father, on the other hand, was an optometrist with three highly productive practices. My mom owned and operated one of the most successful local real estate brokerages. My parents earned quite a few more multiples in income than Sharon and Chuck—you would think that they retired relatively poor.

A few years ago I was skiing with Chuck and their youngest son. It started snowing heavily and we packed it in to the warm bar for a few cold beers—one of those special joys of the ski slopes. I asked Chuck if it was tough to live on the small salary of a retired principal. He gave me an odd look, laughed, then said, *"Hell no, Scott! Sharon made us rich in the stock market! All those years we lived on my salary and once Sharon learned about stocks, she shoveled all of her hair cutting money into the market at just the right time."* Later I had the great pleasure of hearing the details from Sharon. Here is how she did it.

Sharon told me that a high school graduate from the area named Hugh came back from his college studies. He had taken a stock investing seminar and was asking people he knew in the local community to pool their money together. Sharon had been saving money as a beautician and was looking for an investment opportunity, so she threw in with the small pool. Hugh lost all of the money. Sharon laughed and said, *"You know, Scott, I lost twice! Hugh is such a nice guy and when he came around a second time asking for money, I threw away even more money! I wasn't about to allow it to happen a third time and started thinking that maybe I should have a go at it alone."*

The loss was painful to her because both she and her husband lived a frugal lifestyle that revolved around their children. But once bitten by the bug, she developed the resolve to succeed as a stock investor. Providence works in strange ways. Sharon was listening to the radio driving through Los Angeles one day and ran across Bob Brinker's radio show. Bob also has a mutual fund newsletter called MarketTimer (BobBrinker.com). Bob taught Sharon two things that would change her financial life forever. The first was that she had to learn to *"pay herself first."* The second lesson was the financial prudence of dollar cost averaging into no-load mutual funds indexed to the S&P.

Sharon was a quick student. Every time the end of the month came around, she put as much money as she could into her trading account BEFORE she paid anything else— bills, gifts, new televisions, etc. She said the one mistake that she made was that she did not sell out in 2000 at the top of the market even though Bob Brinker was advising his subscribers to do so.

Sharon told me with barely contained excitement in her voice, *"Scott, I was looking at our account balances yesterday and I can't believe how much we are worth!"* I asked, *"But didn't you ride the market down through the worst bear market since the great depression?"* She responded, *"Yes, but before that I rode the market up through the biggest bull market in U.S. history!"* Despite the crash she was still able to retire secure.

You can invest in stocks, bonds, or other financial assets through a mutual fund if you don't want to buy and sell individual stocks on your own actively. **Mutual funds** are nothing more than a way of combining or pooling together money of a large group of investors. The buy and sell decisions for the pool are made by a fund manager who is paid for operating the fund day-to-day.

Mutual funds provide indirect access to financial markets for individual investors; these funds are a form of **financial intermediary**. Mutual funds have a lot of power today because they are now the largest type of financial intermediary in the United States, followed by **commercial banks** and **life insurance companies**.

Trap: Academic studies and market statistics confirm that the typical investor acts in direct opposition to buy low and sell high holding worsening losses and cutting gains short.

At the end of 2001, about 93 million Americans in 55 million households owned mutual funds, up from 5 million households in 1980—this is a huge increase. Investors contributed $505 billion to mutual funds in 2001, and, by the end of the year, mutual fund assets totaled $7 trillion – yes, that's trillion with a "t."

One of the reasons for the explosion in the number of mutual funds and fund types is that mutual funds have become, at a very basic level, consumer products. They are created and marketed to the public in ways that are intended to promote buyer appeal. As every business student knows, product differentiation is a basic marketing tactic, and in recent years mutual funds have become increasingly adept at practicing this crude marketing technique.

In fact, if you are not already a mutual fund investor, it is very likely that you will be in the near future. The reason has to do with a fundamental change in the way businesses of all types provide benefits for employees. It used to be that most large employers offered pension plans. With such a plan, when you retire, your employer pays you a pension typically based on years of service and salary. The key is that the pension payout benefit was "defined" based on a formula.

Defined benefit plans are rapidly being replaced by "**defined contribution plans**." With a defined contribution plan, such as a 401(k), your employer will contribute money each pay period into a retirement account on your behalf based on a defined contribution formula, but you have to select the funds your plan picks. With this arrangement, the benefit you ultimately receive depends entirely on how your investments perform; your employer only makes contributions. The security of your financial retirement is in no way guaranteed. The mutual funds you select could lose your money—lots.

Investment Companies and Fund Types

At the most basic level, a company that pools funds obtained from individual investors and invests them is called an **investment company**. In other words, an investment company is a business that specializes in managing financial assets for individual investors. All **mutual funds** are investment companies, but not all investment companies are mutual funds.

Open-End Versus Closed-End Mutual Funds

There are two types of investment companies, open-end funds and closed-end funds. Whenever you invest in a mutual fund, you do so by buying shares in the fund. However, how your shares are bought and sold depends on which type of fund you are considering.

With an **open-end fund**, the fund itself will sell new shares to anyone wishing to buy and will redeem (another way to say buy back) shares from anyone who wants to sell. When an investor wants to buy open-end fund shares, the fund simply issues the shares and the manager invests the money received from the investor into equity securities. When someone wants to sell open-end fund shares, the manager sells some of its assets and uses the cash to redeem the shares. As a result, with an open-end fund, the number of shares outstanding fluctuates over time.

With a **closed-end fund**, the number of shares is fixed and never changes. If you want to buy shares, you must buy them from another investor. Similarly, if you wish to sell shares that you own, you must sell them to another investor.

The key difference between an open-end fund and a closed-fund is that with a closed-end fund, the fund itself does not buy or sell shares. In fact, shares in closed-end funds are listed on stock exchanges just like ordinary shares of stock, where the fund shares are bought and sold in the same way. Open-end funds are more popular among investors than closed-end funds.

Strictly speaking, the term "mutual fund" actually refers strictly to an open-end investment company. Thus the phrase "closed-end" is an oxymoron, like "jumbo shrimp", and the phrase "open-end mutual fund" is a redundancy, an unnecessary repetition or restatement, such as "past history". Nonetheless, particularly in recent years, the term investment company has all but disappeared from common use, and investment companies are now generically called mutual funds.

Net Asset Value

A mutual fund's **net asset value (NAV)** is calculated by taking the total value of the assets held by the fund less any liabilities divided by the number of outstanding shares. For example, suppose a mutual fund has $105 million in assets, $5 million in liabilities based on current market values and a total of 5 million shares outstanding. Based on the value of net assets held by the fund, $100 million, each share has a value of

$$\frac{\$100\ million}{5\ million\ shares} = \$20\ per\ share = \$20\ NAV$$

This $20 is the fund's net asset value, often abbreviated as **NAV**.

With one important exception, the net asset value of a mutual fund will change substantially every day, simply because the value of the stocks held by the fund go up and down. The one exception concerns money market funds, which I explain below.

An open-end fund will generally redeem shares at any time. The price you receive when you sell your mutual fund shares is the net asset value. In the example above, if you sell your shares back to the fund you will be paid $20 per share. Because the fund stands ready to redeem shares at any time, shares in an open-end fund are always worth their net asset value. In contrast, because the shares of closed-end funds are bought and sold in the stock market, the share price at any point in time may or may not be equal to their net asset values.

MUTUAL FUND OPERATIONS

Mutual funds are created, marketed, and taxed. Each of these topics affects your bottom line as an investor.

Honorable Antonio (Tito) J. Colorado Laguna is the local leading tax attorney. Don Tito served as both Secretary of State and Resident Commissioner of Puerto Rico in the administration of Rafael Hernández Colón.

Mutual Fund Organization and Creation

A mutual fund is simply a corporation. Like a corporation, a mutual fund is owned by its shareholders. The shareholders elect a board of directors. The board of directors is responsible for hiring a manager to oversee the fund's operations. Even though mutual funds often belong to a larger "family" of funds, every fund is a separate company owned by its mutual fund shareholders.

Most mutual funds are created by **investment advisory firms,** which are businesses that specialize in managing mutual funds. Investment advisory firms are also called mutual fund companies. Increasingly, such firms have additional operations such as discount brokerages and other financial services.

There are many investment advisory firms in the United States. The largest and best known is Fidelity Investments, with 150 mutual funds, more than $800 billion in assets under management, and 19 million customers. Dreyfus, Franklin, and Vanguard are some other well-known examples. Many big nationwide brokerage firms, such as Merrill Lynch and Charles Schwab, also have large investment advisory operations.

Investment advisory firms create mutual funds simply because they wish to manage them to earn fees. Fund managers don't care about anything but the fee they earn. Their marketing is oriented toward your benefits and how they strive to protect your interests but reality is different. A typical management fee might be 0.75 percent of the total assets in the fund per year.

A fund would not be especially large with $200 million in assets, but could nonetheless generate management fees of about $1.5 million per year for the manager. It is not hard for you to see why mutual fund managers live in mansions. Here is how a fund is created.

A company like Fidelity might one day decide that there is a demand for a fund that buys stocks in companies to grow and process citrus fruits. Fidelity could form a mutual fund that specializes in such companies and call it something like the Fidelity Lemon Fund. A fund manager would be appointed, and shares in the fund would be offered to the public. As shares are sold, the money received is invested by buying shares of stock in the citrus fruit growing companies. If the fund is a success, a large amount of money will be attracted into the fund and Fidelity will benefit from the fees it earns. If the fund is not a success, the board can vote to liquidate and return the shareholders' money—or merge it with another fund.

As this hypothetical example shows you, an investment advisory firm such as Fidelity can (and often will) create new funds from time to time. Through time, this process leads to a **family of funds** all managed by the same advisory firm. Each fund in the family will have its own fund manager, but the advisory firm will generally handle the record keeping, marketing, and much of the research that underlies the fund's investment decisions.

In principle, the directors of a mutual fund in a particular family, acting on behalf of the fund shareholders, could vote to fire the investment advisory firm and hire a different one. As a practical matter, this rarely, if ever, occurs. At least part of the reason is that the directors are originally appointed by the fund's founder, and are routinely reelected. Unhappy shareholders generally "vote with their feet"—that is, they sell their shares and invest elsewhere when they feel like they have been ripped off by the managers.

Taxation of Investment Companies

As long as an investment company meets certain rules set by the Internal Revenue Code, it is treated as a **"regulated**

investment company" for tax purposes. This is important because a regulated investment company does not pay taxes on its investment income. Instead, the fund passes on these distributions to its shareholders as though they owned the stocks directly. The fund acts as a **"pass-through entity"** in terms of tax law, funneling capital gains and losses to the owners. This can cause problems because you must pay taxes on capital gains of other investors who sold out their shares when the price was higher.

To qualify as a regulated investment company, the fund must follow three basic rules. The first rule is that it must in fact be an investment company holding all of its assets as investments in stocks, bonds, and other securities. The second rule limits the fund to 5% of its assets when acquiring a security. This is called the **five percent rule** of diversification. The third rule is that the fund must pass through all realized investment income to fund shareholders.

The Mutual Fund Prospectus and Annual Report

Mutual funds are required by law to produce a document known as a **prospectus**. The prospectus must be supplied to any investor wishing to purchase shares. Mutual funds must also provide an annual report to their shareholders. The annual report and the prospectus, which are sometimes combined, contain financial statements along with specific information concerning the fund's expenses, gains and losses, holdings, objectives and management.

MUTUAL FUND COSTS AND FEES

Managed mutual funds charge the highest fees in the most confusing manner possible. They do this to suck money out of your pocket. There is a solution for all these nasty fees – buy an index fund.

The Mutual Fund Expense Ratio

A mutual fund's **expense ratio** is the most important fee to understand. The expense ratio is made up of the following. The **investment advisory fee,** or **management fee,** is the money used to pay the salary of the manager(s) of the mutual fund. On average, this fee is about 0.5% to 1.0% of the fund's assets annually.

Another piece of the expense ratio are **administrative costs,** which include things like recordkeeping, mailings, and maintaining a customer service line. These are all necessary costs, though they vary in size from fund to fund. The thriftiest funds can keep these costs below 0.2% of fund assets, while the ones who use engraved paper, colorful graphics, and phone attendants with fancy accents might fail to bring administrative costs below 0.4% of fund assets.

Trap: Hedge funds are notorious for pump-and-dump schemes. Avoid them – or at least go in with your eyes wide open. Watch Wolves of Wall Street for the modern example of Jordan Belfort. Read *The Dhando Investor* for the perspective of the highly regarded and transparent hedge fund manager Mohnish Pabrai who is highly respected by Warren Buffett himself. Available on Amazon.

Avoid the **12b-1 distribution fee**. This fee ranges from 0.25% all the way up to 1.0% of the fund's assets. This fee is spent on marketing, advertising and distribution services. If you're in a fund with a 12b-1 fee, you're paying every year for the fund to run expensive commercials. Can this in any way help you? Do you enjoy seeing advertisements of your fund on television? Unless you do, you should avoid funds that carry a 12b-1 fee.

Don't concern yourself with how the pieces of the expense ratio add up, just know what the total is. The most important question that you should ask about any mutual fund is, *"How high is the expense ratio?"* And remember, for actively managed funds, the average number is about 1.5%. Meanwhile, in the wonderful world of index funds, the expense ratio is six times smaller, around 0.25% and as low as 0.19% for the King Kong cost cutter of all index funds—the Vanguard S&P 500 Index Fund (VFINX). The expense ratio for each publicly traded mutual fund can be found at Morningstar.com.

The Mutual Fund Load

The **"load"** is the sales charge many funds use to pay a stock broker for his or her "services" in selling a fund to an investor. This is loaded on in addition to the expense ratio. **"No-load"** funds are simply those funds that are sold directly to the investor, rather than through a middleman. A **"front-end load"** is a monster chunk of money that a broker or other adviser pays to himself or his company for telling you to buy the fund. Sometimes you will hear these called **A-class shares**. Front-end loads typically congregate around the 5% figure, but can go up to 8%. That means that if you were investing $10,000 in a 5% front load fund, $500 is taken out of your investment account up front and put into the broker's pocket. Don't ever, under any circumstances, buy front-loaded funds.

Deferred load or **contingent deferred sales load (CDSL)** funds (sometimes called **back-end loads**), often labeled **B-class shares**, are just as unnecessarily expensive (bad) as front-end load funds, but they're not as clearly labeled. These funds defer the sales fee until you sell out of the fund.

Level load funds, or **C-class shares**, are a load of trouble. These charge small front loads, and level loads every year thereafter. Although C-class shares might look like they aren't so bad to buy, they end up being very, very expensive to hold because your account gets whacked every year you own the fund.

Mutual Fund Turnover Rate and Taxes

A fund's **turnover rate** is the percentage of a fund's holdings that changes every year as it buys and sells individual stocks or bonds. A managed mutual fund has an average turnover rate of approximately 85%, meaning that funds are selling most of their holdings of stocks or bonds every year. Buying and selling stocks costs money in the form of commissions and bid ask spreads, so a high turnover indicates higher costs (and lower shareholder returns) for the fund. Also, funds that have large turnover ratios will end up distributing short-term capital gains to their shareholders annually, even when the fund loses money. Shareholders must pay taxes on these phantom gains, and paying these taxes is a return killer. You can lose money in a managed mutual fund by the end of the year AND get a bill for phantom capital gains tax. Keep a close eye on the turnover rate of any fund you own. Buy funds with low turnover rates. Index fund turnover is around 5% at most, and frequently lower.

Load vs. No Load

Back in 1980 when I graduated from high school, investors could only buy directly through a stockbroker. That meant that all mutual funds were "load" funds. The advent of online discount brokerages made it really easy for mutual funds to sell directly to you cutting out stock brokers as sales people. The stock brokerages started losing commissions, so they teamed up with the mutual funds and invented A-, B-, and C-class share funds to confuse more money out of you. Index funds have the lowest expense ratios, so buy an index fund in your retirement account rather than class share funds. If you have to buy a mutual fund, as you are forced to in an employer sponsored 401(k), just buy a no-load index fund with the very lowest expense ratio (the Vanguard 500 is a great one). If your sponsored 401(k) or **403(b)** doesn't give you the choice of an indexed mutual fund you have a cruddy employer plan.[28] You don't need to pay an adviser to find a mutual fund for you.

Lucy Crespo is the executive director of the Puerto Rico Science Trust working with Dr. Brown to commercialize patents arising from The University of Puerto Rico scientific research.

---

[28] A 403(b) is a retirement plan like a 401(k) plan, but is offered by non-profit organizations, such as universities and some charitable entities, rather than corporations. There are several advantages to 403(b) plans: contributions lower taxable income, larger contributions can be made to the account, earnings can grow tax-deferred, and some plans allow loans. Contributions can grow tax-deferred until withdrawal at which time the money is taxed as ordinary income (which is sometimes a disadvantage).

Studies show that no-load funds perform better than, load funds. Buy no-load funds. If you're in a 401(k) or 403(b) plan, make sure you know whether the fund choices offered are load or no-load—that information may not be contained in one-sheet summaries of fund choice performance. Take the list and go to *Morningstar.com* to check the loads, fees and so forth.

Mutual Fund Morningstar Stars

Don't pay any attention whatsoever to the "stars" you see associated with mutual funds and their advertisements. The premier mutual fund data provider, Morningstar, assigns stars on the basis of subjectively assessed risk and return—attempting to compare one fund with other funds that have similar investment objectives. But objectives don't reflect fund composition. Morningstar's rating system is totally meaningless.

Selecting Mutual Funds

Selecting the best fund is easy. Buy an index fund. Index funds are available for international stocks, growth stocks, mid-caps, small-caps, and just about anything else you can think of. My favorite for any employer sponsored 401(k) is the Vanguard 500 fund (VFINX) if available as a menu selection. If you are forced to buy a non-index fund, make sure that you understand all the costs and fees associated with buying and owning that fund. Check the long-term chart patterns on all of them.

LONG-TERM FUNDS

There are many different types of long-term mutual funds. Historically, mutual funds were classified as stock, bond or income funds. The rapid growth in mutual funds has made it increasingly difficult to place all funds into just these three categories. Also, providers of mutual fund information do not use the same classification schemes. Mutual funds have different goals, and a fund's objective is the major determinant of the fund type.

All mutual funds must state the fund's objective in the prospectus. For example, the *"Fidelity Independence Fund"* states:

> *"The fund's objective is capital appreciation. Normally, the fund's strategy is to invest primarily in common stocks of domestic and foreign issue. The fund strategy may result in the realization of capital gains without considering tax consequences to shareholders. Fidelity Management & Research Company (FMR) is not constrained by any particular investment style and may invest in "growth" stocks, "value" stocks, or both, at any given time."*

Trap: Do not, under any circumstances, buy shares of your employer's company stock in your 401(k) plan. If the company goes bankrupt, you will lose your retirement – as did Enron and World-Com employees!

This fund says it invests in different types of stocks with the goal of capital appreciation. This is clearly a stock fund, and it might further be classified as a "capital appreciation" fund or an "aggressive growth" fund, depending on whose classification scheme is used.

Mutual fund objectives are an important consideration; unfortunately, the truth is that, like the Fidelity objective above, they are too vague to provide useful information as is. For example, it is very common that the objective reads like this: *"The Big Bucks Fund seeks capital appreciation, income, and capital preservation."* Translation: The fund seeks to (1) increase the value of its shares, (2) generate income for its shareholders, and (3) not lose money—important sounding useless information! More to the point, funds with very similar sounding objectives can have very different portfolios and, hence, very different risks. Thus, it is a mistake to focus on a mutual fund's stated objective. Actual portfolio holdings speak louder than prospectus promises. These promises are hollow lies designed by marketing hacks to suck your money into the black hole of an expensive mutual fund.

Stock Funds

Stock funds exist in great variety. I'll explain to you nine separate general types and some subtypes. I'll also show you some new types that don't fit neatly into any category. You don't need to bother with any of this if you just buy a no-load indexed mutual fund.

The first four types of stock funds trade off capital appreciation with dividend income.

1. **Capital appreciation stock mutual funds** seek maximum capital appreciation —a fancy way of saying that they try to sell higher than they buy. They generally invest in companies that have, in the opinion of the fund manager, the best prospects for share price appreciation without regard to dividends, company size, or, for some funds, country of origin. Often this means investing in unproven companies or companies perceived out-of-favor.

2. **Growth stock mutual funds** seek capital appreciation, but tend to invest in large, more established companies. These funds may be somewhat less volatile

as a result. Dividends are an important consideration for the mutual fund manager in purchasing a stock.

3. **Growth and income stock mutual funds** seek capital appreciation, but at least part of their focus is on dividend-paying companies.

4. **Equity income stock mutual funds** focus almost exclusively on stocks with relatively high dividend yields, thereby maximizing the current income on the stock portfolio.[29]

Among these four fund types, the greater the emphasis on growth, the greater the supposed risk, at least as a general rule. Again, these are rough classifications. Equity income funds, for example, frequently invest heavily in public utility stocks, which suffered heavy losses at the beginning of the 1990s.

Company size-based stock mutual funds focus on companies in a particular size range.

1. **Small company stock mutual funds** focus on stocks in small companies where "small" refers to the total market value of the stock. Such funds are often called "small-cap" funds, where "cap" is short for total market value, also called market capitalization. Small stocks have historically performed very well, at least over the long run, hence the high demand for funds that specialize in small cap stocks. With small-company mutual funds, what constitutes small covers a wide range of companies from perhaps $10 million up to $1 billion or so in total market value, and some funds specialize in smaller companies than

---

[29] The **dividend yield** is the anticipated dividend divided by the present price of a share of stock.

others. Since most small companies don't pay dividends, these funds by definition emphasize capital appreciation.

2. **Midcap stock mutual funds** specialize in stocks that are too small to be in the S&P 500 index, but too large to be considered small stocks. Hence, the stocks these mutual funds specialize in are considered to be middle- or medium-sized by market capitalization, a.k.a. midcap.

International stock mutual funds invest internationally. International funds have been among the most rapidly growing funds. However, that growth slowed sharply in the late 1990s.

1. **Global stock mutual funds** have substantial international holdings, but also maintain significant investments in U.S. stocks.

2. **International stock mutual funds** are just like global funds, except they focus on non-U.S. equities.

Among international funds, some specialize in specific regions of the world, such as Europe, the Pacific Rim or South America. Others specialize in individual countries. Today, there is at least one mutual fund specializing in essentially every country in the world that has a stock market, however small.

International funds that specialize in countries with small or recently established stock markets are often called **emerging market funds**. Almost all single-country funds, and especially emerging market funds, are not diversified and have historically had extremely volatile returns to investors—a lot of up and down surprise price movements. Make sure you

Tip: Only contribute up to the maximum matching in an employer sponsored 401(k). After that, save into a Roth IRA or Roth Solo K. If you are worried about your financial stability, then the Roth IRA and Roth Solo K is for you. You can withdraw the contribution in an emergency penalty free — you get heavily penalized for early withdrawals in a 401(k).

understand the stock market of the country these mutual funds are invested in. The best newspaper to track foreign markets is the *Christian Science Monitor*. Don't worry about its religious-sounding name, because it is not a religious newspaper. Smart economists like Kissinger at schools like Harvard University read it because it is less biased by corporate or U.S. political interests.[30]

Many funds classified as international funds may actually have substantial overseas investments, so this is one thing to watch out for. It is not unusual for a fund to call itself a "growth" fund and actually invest heavily outside the United States borders.

Other Stock Mutual Fund Types and Issues

There are three other types of stock mutual funds that don't fit easily into a category.

1. **Index stock mutual funds** simply buy and hold the stocks that make up an index in the same proportions. The most important index funds are the **S&P 500 indexed stock mutual funds** which are intended to track the performance of the S&P 500—one of the largest stock indexes. By their nature, index funds are

---

[30] For a subscription to the Christian Science Monitor newspaper go to www.csmonitor.com

passively managed, meaning that the fund manager uses a computer program to trade as necessary to match the index. Such funds are appealing because of low turnover and miserly operating expenses. Another reason index funds have grown so rapidly is that there is considerable debate over whether active mutual fund managers can consistently beat the averages—empirical studies by top financial economists indicate that they can't. And if they can't, then why pay loads and management fees when it's cheaper to buy the averages by indexing?

2. **Social conscience stock mutual funds** are a relatively new creation. They invest only in companies whose products, policies, or politics are considered to be socially desirable. Social objectives range from environmental issues to personnel policies. The **Parnassus Fund** is a great example because it avoids the alcoholic beverage, tobacco, gambling, weapons and nuclear power industries. Of course, general agreement on what is socially desirable or responsible is hard to find. In fact, there are so-called **sin stock mutual funds** (and sector funds) that specialize in what Parnassus fund shareholders would consider "sinful" industries!

3. **Tax-managed stock mutual funds** are managed with high regard for your tax liabilities as a mutual fund shareholder. Normally, fund managers focus on total pretax returns because this is what their performance bonus is based on. Recent research has shown that some very simple strategies can greatly improve your after-tax returns. Focusing on pretax returns is not a good idea for investors. Tax-managed stock mutual funds hold turnover down to minimize realized short-term capital gains. Managers pair

realized short-term gains with realized short-term losses (short term is owning a stock for less than a year). These tax saving strategies work well for index funds. For example, the **Schwab 1000 Fund** is a fund that tracks the Russell 1000 index, a widely followed 1,000-stock index. However, the fund will deviate from exactly following the index to avoid realizing short-term taxable gains. As a result, the fund holds turnover down to a minimum. Fund shareholders are shielded from short-term capital gains taxes as a result. Funds promoting such tax saving strategies will become common if investors become aware of the tax consequences if forced to invest outside of a 401(k), Roth IRA, or Roth 401(k).

Taxable and Municipal Bond Mutual Funds

If you have a 401(k) sponsored by your employer, you have probably been enticed to put part of your money into a bond fund to diversify. This is a very bad move because bond funds do not have a maturity. You would be much better off if you could just buy the bonds the fund owns outright because you could lock in the interest (yield) for the length of the maturity you want. But your 401(k) doesn't give you that choice. The big problem with a bond mutual fund in a rising interest rate market is that a bond is worth less as the interest rate rises. If you buy a bond at 5%, you will pay $1,000 and get $50 every year. If the interest rate rises to 6% and you want to sell your bond before maturity, you have a problem because someone with $1,000 to invest in bonds will get $60. This means that you will have to sell your bond for less than $1,000—your bonds lose value when interest rates rise. As bond mutual fund managers try to lock in higher and higher rates, they end up selling the bonds they bought in the past with your bond mutual fund contributions in your employer sponsored 401(k). This means that you will start to lose money as interest rates rise because you can't simply tell the bond mutual fund manager not to sell the bonds he bought with your money. Nonetheless, investors in bond funds were much better off in the stock market crash from 2000 to 2003 because they did not lose much while many stock mutual funds lost well over half their value. Do not buy bond funds. Buy one stock index fund in an employer sponsored 401(k) or buy a ladder of bonds one-by-one in a self-directed Roth and Roth Solo K.

Balanced mutual funds that buy both stocks and bonds are even worse. Two famous financial economists found that if a 401(k) plan offers a choice between a stock fund and a bond fund, most people simply put 50% into each fund, reasoning that the fixed income of bonds will offset the risk of unknown price changes in stocks—they think that they are diversifying.[31] Most 401(k) plans offer balanced funds which are composed of half stocks and bonds. Shlomo Benartzi and Richard Thaler found that people put 50% in a stock mutual fund and 50% in a balanced mutual fund.

Without realizing it, many investors are putting 75% of their employer sponsored 401(k) investment in stock and 25% in bonds.

Tip: The Roth IRA is self-directed, judgment-proof, and probate-free. This means that you get to pick your own stock, don't lose it if someone sues you, and your kids don't have to cut it up with the government when you pass.

---

[31] Benartzi, Shlomo, and Richard Thaler, "Naive Diversification Strategies in Retirement Saving Plans," American Economic Review, March 2001, Vol. 91.1, pp. 79-98.

Most bond funds invest in domestic corporate and government securities. Some invest in foreign government and non-U.S. corporate bonds as well. As you will see, there are not a lot of bond fund types. Here are the five characteristics that help you tell them apart:

1. **Maturity range**. Different funds hold bonds of different maturities, ranging from very short (2 years) to quite long (25-30 years).

2. **Credit quality**. Some bonds are much safer than others in terms of the possibility of default where payments to you stop. U.S. Treasury bonds (T-bonds) have never defaulted in the history of the country and hence are considered risk-free. T-bonds don't have default risk because the United States Treasury can print more dollars as needed to repay investors. On the other hand, so-called junk bonds have lots of default risk. Since the payments on junk bonds may stop at any time, these bonds pay higher yields to compensate you for the high risk. Do not chase yield without considering how to manage your risk.

3. **Taxability**. Municipal bond funds buy bonds that are free from state and local income tax. Taxable bond funds buy taxable issues.

4. **Type of bond**. Some funds specialize in particular types of fixed-income instruments such as mortgages.

5. **Country**. Most bond funds buy just domestic issues, but some buy foreign corporate and government bonds.

Short and intermediate-term bond mutual funds focus on a specific maturity range. Short-term maturities are generally bonds that make the last payment to the bond fund within five years from when you invest. Intermediate-term bonds pay in full within 10 years. There are both taxable and municipal bond funds with these maturity targets.

Be very careful of the credit quality of the bonds from fund to fund. One fund could hold very risky intermediate term junk bonds while another might hold low risk U.S. government issues with similar maturities.

General bond mutual funds are a catch-all for bond funds that hold both taxable and municipal debt. Funds in this category simply don't specialize. Maturities can vary as well. My warning to you about the varied credit quality of the bonds in these funds means that you must beware as to what you are buying.

High-yield municipal and taxable bond mutual funds specialize in low-credit quality issues, like bonds sold

Mohnish Pabrai, the third most famous value investor in the world behind Buffett and Munger talks stocks with Dr. Brown's UPR-RP MBA corporate finance students.

by Orange County in California that went bankrupt.[32] These bond issues have higher yields because of the greater risk that you may not get paid. As a result, *"high-yield"* bond mutual funds can be very volatile.

Mortgage mutual funds specialize in mortgage backed securities (MBS) such as the Government National Mortgage Association (GNMA also known as Ginny Mae) issues. There are no municipal mortgage-backed securities yet so these are all taxable bond funds.

World bond mutual funds invest worldwide and are few in number. Some specialize in foreign government issues while others buy a variety of non-U.S. issues. These are all taxable funds.

Insured mutual bond funds are a type of municipal bond fund. Municipal bond issuers frequently purchase insurance that guarantees the bond's payments will be made. Such bonds have very little possibility of default, so some funds specialize in them.

Single-state municipal bond funds specialize in issues from a single state. These are especially important in states like California that have high state and municipal tax rates.

---

[32] In December 1994, Orange County stunned the markets by announcing that its investment pool had suffered a loss of $1.6 billion. This was the largest default ever recorded by a local government, and led to the bankruptcy of the county shortly thereafter. This loss was the result of the unsupervised investment activity of Bob Citron, the County Treasurer, who was entrusted with a $7.5 billion portfolio belonging to county schools, cities, special districts and the county itself. In times of fiscal restraints, Citron was viewed as a wizard who could painlessly deliver greater returns to investors. Indeed, Citron delivered returns about 2% higher than the comparable State pool before this financial disaster was revealed.

Confusingly, this classification refers only to long-term funds. Short and intermediate single-state funds are classified with other maturity-based municipal funds.

Stock and Bond Funds

This last group includes a variety of funds. The only common feature is that these don't invest exclusively in either stocks or bonds. For this reason, they are often called "**blended**" or "**hybrid**" funds.

Balanced stock and bond mutual funds maintain a relatively fixed split between stocks and bonds. They emphasize relatively safe, high-quality investments. Such funds provide a kind of "one-stop shopping" for fund investors, particularly smaller investors, because they diversify into both stocks and bonds.

Asset allocation stock and bond mutual funds come in two flavors. The first is an extended version of a balanced fund that holds relatively fixed proportional investments in stocks, bonds, money market instruments, and perhaps real estate or some other investment class. The target proportions may be updated or modified periodically.

The other type of asset allocation fund is often called a **flexible portfolio fund**. Here, the fund manager may hold up to 100% in stocks, bonds, or money market instruments, depending on his or her views about the likely performance of these investments. These funds essentially try to time the market, guessing which general type of investment will do well (or less poorly) over the months ahead.

Convertible stock and bond mutual funds can be swapped for a fixed number of shares of stock at the option of the shareholder. Some mutual funds specialize in these bonds.

Income stock and bond funds emphasize generating dividend and coupon (bond interest) income on investments. These hold a variety of dividend-paying common, as well as preferred, stocks and bonds of various maturities.

Research the composition of the fund—what stock or bonds it holds in its portfolio.[33] Lipper, Inc. is a helpful company that tracks mutual fund composition: *lipperweb.com*.

MUTUAL FUND PERFORMANCE

Mutual fund performance is tracked very closely by a large number of organizations. If you look at performance ratings in the Wall Street Journal, you would wonder why anyone would buy a fund other than those mutual funds with the highest returns. This is a bad strategy. If the market has done well, the best ranked fund may be the riskiest. In a market downturn, the best ranked funds are most likely to become the worst ranked funds.

There is an even more fundamental criterion. Ultimately, you don't care about historical performance; you care about future performance. Many of the poorest performing funds have the highest costs. These costs act as a constant drag on the mutual fund's performance and your bottom line, and have persistently poorer returns than otherwise similar funds. Stick to no-load indexed mutual funds or equivalent ETFs.

---

[33] A portfolio is a collection of investments all owned by the same individual or organization. These investments often include stocks, which are investments in individual businesses; bonds, which are investments in debt that are designed to earn interest; and mutual funds, which are essentially pools of money from many investors that are invested by professionals or according to indices.

Money Market Funds

Some investors use money market funds to park money. A unique feature of **money market fund accounting** is that the net asset values are $1 per share. A money market fund simply sets the number of shares equal to the fund's assets. In other words, if the fund earns $100 million in

Trap: Do not buy bond funds and especially so when interest rates are rising—that is when they lose value!

assets, then it has 100 million shares. Investors are given more shares as the fund reinvests interest received from money market investments.

The reason that a money market fund maintains a $1 net asset value is to make them resemble bank savings accounts. As long as a money market fund invests in very safe, interest-bearing, short-maturity assets, its net asset value will not drop below $1 per share. However, there is no guarantee that this won't happen, and the term **"breaking the buck"** is used to describe the fund's share price dropping below $1 in net asset value. This is a very rare situation, but, in 1994, several large money market funds experienced substantial losses because they purchased relatively risky derivative assets (stock options are a derivative asset, for example) and broke the buck—so it can happen. Not only can it happen, it did again in 2007.

Money market funds are either taxable or tax-exempt. Taxable funds are more common; of the $2.3 trillion in total money market fund assets in 2003, taxable funds accounted for about 87 percent. As a general rule, interest earned on state and local government securities (called **"municipal**

securities") are exempt from federal income tax. Non-taxable money market funds buy these types of tax-exempt securities.

Some tax exempt securities go further. Interest paid by one state is often subject to another state's taxes depending on where the mutual fund shareholder lives. Therefore, some tax-exempt funds buy securities issued by a single state. For residents of that state, the interest earned is both federal and state tax-exempt. For beleaguered New York City residents, there are **triple-tax-free money market funds** that invest in New York City obligations, thereby allowing the residents to escape federal, state and metropolitan income taxes on the interest earned.

Tax exempt money market instruments pay much lower **yields** (interest rates) due to favorable tax treatment. For example, in mid-2003, taxable money market mutual funds offered about a 1.2% yield, whereas tax-exempt funds offered just 0.9%. Which is better depends on your individual tax bracket. If you're in a 40% bracket, then the taxable fund is paying a $(0.12)(1-0.40)= 0.0072 = 0.72\%$ yield after-tax—you're better off with the tax-exempt fund.

Money Market Deposit Accounts

Most banks offer what are called **money market deposit accounts (MMDAs)**, which are a lot like money market mutual funds. For example, both money market funds and money market deposit accounts generally have limited check writing privileges. There is a very important distinction between a bank-offered money market account and a money market fund. A **bank money market** account is a bank deposit offering FDIC protection,[34] whereas a money

---

[34] The Federal Deposit Insurance Corporation (FDIC) is a federal agency that insures deposits in member banks and thrifts up to $100,000.

market fund does not. A money market fund will generally offer SIPC protection,[35] but this is a poor substitute for FDIC protection because it does not insure against investment losses, such as if an MMDA "breaks the buck" for mishandling the fund investment portfolio. Confusingly, some banks offer both money market accounts and, through a separate entity, money market funds. A money market account with FDIC protection is much, much better than a money market fund with SIPC protection!

CLOSED-END FUNDS, EXCHANGE TRADED FUNDS, AND HEDGE FUNDS

Closed end funds have some weird things worth knowing.

Closed End funds

The major difference between a closed-end fund and an open-end fund, is that closed end funds don't buy and sell shares. Instead, there are a fixed number of shares in the fund, and these shares are bought and sold on the open market. About 450 closed-end funds have their shares traded on U.S. stock exchanges, which is far fewer than the approximately 7,000 long-term, open-end mutual funds available to investors today in 2006.

The Closed-End Fund Discount Mystery

Wall Street has many unsolved puzzles. One of the most famous and enduring has to do with the price of shares in

---

[35] The Securities Investor Protection Corporation (SIPC) is a non-profit membership corporation established by Congress which insures securities and cash in customer accounts up to $500,000 (up to $100,000 on cash) in the event of brokerage bankruptcy. The SIPC is funded by all member securities broker/dealers. While it insures the account if a brokerage runs out of funds to cover its claims, it does not, however, insure against investment losses.

closed-end funds. Shares in closed-end funds trade in the market place. Share prices can differ from their net asset values in a very strange way. Perplexingly, most closed-end funds sell at a discount to their net asset values, and the discount is sometimes substantial!

For example, suppose a closed-end stock mutual fund owns $100 million of stock. The fund itself has 10 million shares outstanding. The NAV is $10. It is not unusual for the share price to trade at $9; a discount of 10%. What is puzzling is that an investor can purchase $10 worth of stock for just $9!

Even more puzzling is that the typical discount fluctuates over time. Sometimes the discount is very wide; at other times, it almost disappears. Despite a great deal of research, the closed-end fund discount phenomenon remains completely unexplained.

Carlos Vila, JD, MBA (UPR-RP Law and Finance) queries Mohnish Pabrai and Secretary Bacó regarding value investing in the stock market.

Because of the discount on closed-end funds beginning investors are attracted to those with the largest discounts. The problem with this logic is that it assumes that the discount will narrow or disappear. Unfortunately, this may or may not happen; the discount might grow wider.

Avoid IPOs of closed-end funds. When a closed-end fund goes public, its shares are offered without a discount. Using the example above, you would have to buy the IPO shares at $10. You will lose in two ways. First, the fund promoter will be paid a hefty chunk, perhaps 7% off of the top from the proceeds, or about $7 million in this example (this will be disclosed in the prospectus). The problem is that this fee will come out of money in the fund, leaving a total value of $93 million and an NAV of $9.30. Second, the shares will then drop in value to reflect the discount relative to the NAV in the market. You would lose another piece of your investment almost immediately. In short, closed-end funds are to be avoided as poor investments.

Exchange Traded Funds

Exchange traded funds (ETFs) are a recent financial innovation. They have been around since 1993, but they really began to grow in the late 1990s. As of 2003, there were over 100 traded ETFs. Basically, an ETF is akin to an indexed mutual fund. When you buy an ETF, you are buying the particular basket of stocks of an index. For example, the best known ETF is the **Standard and Poor's Depository Receipt (SPDR)**, pronounced **"spider"**, which simply buys the S&P 500 index.

What makes an ETF different from an index fund is that an ETF trades like a closed-end fund without the return haircut. ETFs can be bought and sold during the day and can also be sold short. They generally have very low expenses—lower even than index funds—but you have to pay a commission to buy and sell shares.

The fact that ETFs trade like shares in closed-end funds raises the possibility that they could sell at a discount to the net asset values, but this probably won't happen. The fund will buy and sell directly like an open-end fund, but there is a minimum purchase size of 50,000 shares. Furthermore, an ETF will redeem shares in-kind, meaning that if you sell a block of 50,000 shares to the fund, you actually receive the underlying stock instead of cash. So, if an ETF were to sell for a discount, big investors would buy up the shares, redeem them in exchange for the stock, and then sell the stock, thereby capturing the discount without taking any risk. This kind of buying and selling that ensures that ETFs will probably never trade at a discount is arbitrage.

Arbitrage is a risk-free activity that involves buying and selling a security such as a stock, futures contract, option, or ETF to take advantage of a price difference between two markets at the same time. In plain language, if a company's stock is selling for $12 on the NYSE and $9 on the AMEX, then **arbitrageurs**—people who do arbitrage—will buy the stock on the AMEX and sell the same stock on the NYSE for as much as they can as fast as they can. Buying on the AMEX exchange will push the price up. Selling on the NYSE will cause the price on that exchange to fall until the level is the same on each exchange. Arbitrage keeps prices in line by forcing **price convergence**—a uniform price for the same asset, such as a stock. This is also known as the **law of one price**.

Which is better, an ETF or a traditional index fund? It's hard to say. For an index like the S&P 500, it probably doesn't make much difference. However, one place ETFs have an edge is with some of the more specialized indexes I discussed before. For example, ETFs provide a very cheap way of purchasing non-U.S. indexes. Similarly, there are ETFs that track industry indexes for which few ordinary index funds are available. Others allow you to control commodities or foreign currencies.

Like any investment, ETFs aren't appropriate for everyone in every situation. Here is a rundown of the pros. You have a lot more flexibility than in a mutual fund because ETFs are listed on an exchange – you can buy and sell them at whatever share price they happen to be trading during the day just like shares of stocks. Because they trade like stocks, you can buy ETF options in hopes of magnifying your gains. You can also use techniques for profiting from market downturns such as selling short with puts—which involves a contract for the option of borrowing shares and selling them in the hopes of replacing them with less expensive shares when the market falls. I don't recommend shorting, but it is possible to short ETFs. The ETF's biggest positive is low annual operating costs. The Vanguard 500 Fund (VFINX) expenses are not only well below those of traditional mutual funds, but in many cases, even less than the expenses levied by their index fund counterparts.

For example, the iShares S&P 500 ETF charges 0.09 percent of assets per year, or just $18 a year on a $20,000 investment, while the Vanguard Total Stock Market VIPER, an ETF that tracks the entire U.S. stock market including stocks large and small, carries annual operating fees of just 0.07% of assets, or just $14 a year on a $20,000 investment. ETFs trade on an exchange like stocks, which means you're buying shares from or selling them to another ETF investor. So the ETF itself doesn't have to buy or sell securities, meaning there are no taxable gains to be passed on. ETFs may still generate taxable gains, however, if they have to sell shares to reflect a change in the stocks that make up the index they track. And like any other mutual fund, an ETF must pass along interest and dividend payments it receives. The important thing to remember, though, is that you are dealing with the share price, not the NAV, and you know exactly what your tax consequences are.

Fact: The bond market is far greater in size than the stock market! In 2003, the global bond market was worth $43 trillion as compared to $27 trillion in stock.

Here are the cons to investing in an ETF. Probably the biggest disadvantage to ETFs is that you've got to buy them through a broker. If you buy through an online discount brokerage, then these commissions are minimized—unless you are dollar cost averaging with small amounts of money. Even with the low fees available at discount and online brokers these days, brokerage commissions seriously erode an ETF's low-expense advantage, especially when investing small sums of money. If this is the case, you will have to wait for enough capital to pile up in your investment account to offset the brokerage commission. For example, if you were planning to invest, say, $100 a month in ETFs, a cost of just $10 per trade would mean 10% of your investment is being siphoned off. So your ETF's price would have to rise 10% just to recoup your buying cost—and you'll have to pay a commission when you sell, too.

For this reason alone, ETFs are better for investors who are socking away large amounts of money in Roth IRA and Roth 401(k) [a.k.a. Roth Solo K] self-directed plans. If you're dollar cost averaging with small sums or you tend to invest sporadically with modest amounts of money, you're better off in an indexed mutual fund rather than the corresponding ETF.

You could be tempted to try jumping into sectors of the market you believe are about to explode for gains and then bail out just before the sector tanks since you can very easily move in and out of ETFs quickly. This is called **sector timing**. This may seem like a great strategy in theory. In reality, it's a difficult feat to pull off. Many investors end up buying into hot sectors late after prices have been bid up and then find themselves selling for a loss after the sector flames out. Even if you manage to time your entry and exit correctly, there's still the matter of transaction costs, which can eat into potential returns. Research by finance professor Terrance Odean of Cal Berkeley Haas School of Business shows that the more often individual investors trade, the worse they tend to do.[36]

Hedge Funds

Hedge funds are a special type of investment company. These firms are like mutual funds in that a fund manager invests a pool of money for investors and takes his fee off the top. However, unlike mutual funds, hedge funds are not required to register with the SEC. They are only lightly regulated and are generally free to pursue

Fact: One of the most popular ETFs is the NASDAQ-100 —symbol QQQQ. Many people also trade options on this ETF.

---

[36] Odean, T., *"Do Investors Trade Too Much?"*, American Economic Review, 1999, Volume 89, Issue 5, 1279-1298

almost any investment style they wish. In contrast, mutual funds are regulated and are relatively limited in their permitted investment strategies. For example, mutual funds are not allowed to do things like sell short or use a high degree of leverage.

Hedge funds are not required to maintain any degree of diversification or liquidity.[37] They don't have to redeem shares on demand, and they have little in the way of disclosure requirements. **Disclosure** is simply the release of relevant information. The reason that hedge funds avoid many of the restrictions placed on mutual funds is that they only accept "financially sophisticated" investors, and they do not offer their securities for sale to the public. A financially sophisticated investor is, as a practical matter, usually either an institution or a high net worth (rich) individual. Some types of hedge funds are limited to no more than 100 investors.

Hedge funds typically have a special cost structure, where, in addition to a general management fee of one to two percent of fund assets, the manager is paid a special performance fee. This special performance fee is often in the range of 20% to 40% of profits realized by the fund's investment strategy. A modest fee structure might be one that charges an annual management fee of 1% of the fund's assets plus 20%

---

[37] **Diversification** is a portfolio strategy designed to reduce exposure to risk by combining a variety of investments, such as stocks, bonds, and real estate, which are unlikely to move in the same price direction simultaneously. The goal of diversification is to reduce the risk in a portfolio. Volatility is limited by the fact that not all asset classes or industries or individual companies move up and down in value at the same time or at the same rate. Diversification reduces both the upside and downside potential and supposedly allows for more consistent performance over a wide range of economic conditions—Warren Buffet calls diversification, *"an excuse for not thinking!"*

of any profits realized—even more elaborate fee structures are common.

Worldwide, there are thousands of hedge funds, and the number keeps growing. Big hedge funds may require a minimum investment of $1 million or more. Small hedge funds may require $50,000 or less. Whether large or small, each fund develops its own investment style or niche. For example, a hedge fund may focus on a particular sector, like technology, or a particular global region, like Asia or Eastern Europe.

Alternatively, a hedge fund may pursue a "market neutral strategy" in which the fund maintains a portfolio split between long and short positions. The portfolio is hedged against market risk long in some securities, short in others and said to be "market neutral". Incidentally, this is often thought to be the source of the term "hedge fund," originally referring to funds that were hedged against market risk. Today, however, the term hedge fund refers to any unregistered investment fund pursuing any type of investment style offered as private placements under SEC Regulation D to accredited and qualified investors.

Ever dreamed of becoming an investment portfolio manager? You can by starting your own hedge fund. It may be easier than you think. A hedge fund is typically structured as a limited partnership in which the manager is the general partner and the investors are limited partners. Rather than drag you through the legal details, just know you will need the services of a lawyer specialized in investment companies if you decide to create a hedge fund. My point here is that it is not difficult to do. Really, the hardest part about starting your own hedge fund is finding private capital. Essentially, you need to find well-to-do individuals—accredited investors—who have faith in your investment ideas.

Chapter 5: The Language of Stock Options!

Captain Bob is a senior pilot for US Airways. I watched inside corporate executives strip his family of everything Americans hold dear and true. Bob was one of the winners in a first-world economy and an example of the American Dream. That is, until inside corporate America stole his income, his defined benefit plan, and ultimately his pension piece by piece.

Before I lunge into Captain Bob's personal account, let me give you a brief financial history of fear and loathing at US Airways headquarters. First, a brief background in management theory. **Peter Drucker,** who died at the age of 95, is often called the father of corporate management. Drucker's most significant contribution is that he recognized the role of the worker in corporate success. He considered the knowledge of a good employee to be the most significant asset of the firm. Most importantly, he preached the importance of managing employees in a corporate community based on trust and respect. I wonder what opinion he would have today about the stewardship of US Airways ex-CEO David Siegel, who made sure his family's medical coverage was guaranteed for life while he stripped 28,000 US Airways employees and 18,800 retirees of their health coverage in his last year at the helm before skipping town in 2004?

There are real concerns about an insane upward spiral of CEO paycheck sizes. Even back in 1984, Drucker felt that

CEO compensation was out of control. He recommended that it be limited to 20 times the salary of the average worker in the company. By 1991, the average large-corporation CEO earned about 140 times the pay of the common employee. And by 2003, the same CEO earned 500 times the rank and file salary.[38] Inside corporate executives also receive huge severance packages called **golden parachutes** when they lose their jobs.

Are you thinking, "How much does this cost me as a shareholder?"

In 1993, the top five executives of U.S. public companies siphoned away 4.8% of company profits. By 2003, they were able to pirate away 10.3% of the earnings of the companies they "managed." The total a decade later was roughly $290 billion – ten times the 2005 discretionary budget for the Department of Homeland Security![39]

There is also the problem of **unprofitable mergers**. Did you know that senior inside executives get more money when they buy a new company or sell their current one as long as they negotiate the deal? They make a pile of money when they close the sale or merger of the company they manage and get another pile of money—a golden parachute—for

---

[38] Bebchuk, Lucian Arye and Fried, Jesse M., "Executive Compensation as an Agency Problem" . Journal of Economic Perspectives, Vol. 17, Summer 2003

[39] Lucian Bebchuk and Yaniv Grinstein, "The Growth in Executive Pay" (Discussion Draft, 2005) ("During this period [1993-2003], pay has grown much beyond the increase that could be explained by changes in firm size, performance and industry classification. Had the relationship of compensation to size, performance and industry classification remained the same in 2003 as it was in 1993, mean compensation in 2003 would have been only about half of its actual size.")

losing their job. Can you see the serious conflict of interest with the shareholders?

Executive Insider	Deal	Booty
James Kilts	2005 Gillette – P&G merger	$153 million
John Zeglis	2004 AT&T Wireless sale	$32 million
David Dorman	2004 AT&T Wireless sale	$10.3 million
Top AT&T Executives	2004 AT&T Wireless sale	$31 million
Wallace Barr	2005 Caesar's sale	$20 million

Another problem is that inside executives get paid even if the company crashes. The year before Refco sold shares to the public—and immediately made the fourth-largest bankruptcy filing in U.S. history—insiders at the firm sucked away more than $1 billion from the company. The top three executives at Viacom—CEO Summer Redstone and co-presidents Tom Freston and Leslie Moonves—received a total compensation of $160 million in 2005. Viacom then lost $17.5 billion as its share price fell 18%. Corporate corruption, however, is not strictly a male trait. Hewlett-Packard paid outgoing CEO Carly Fiorina a severance package of $21 million—within a month HP paid incoming CEO Mark Hurd a $20 million "welcoming package." Former Disney President Michael Ovitz made $140 million in 1996 after only 14 months on the job. US Airways CEO David Siegal collected $4.5 million upon leaving after placing the carrier in its second bankruptcy. Procter & Gamble CEO Durk Jager left the company with a package in excess of $9.5 million after overseeing a 55% drop in share price. Morgan Stanley's former CEO Phillip Purcell was due to receive $62 million in retirement, yet was also paid an additional $44 million plus administrative support and executive medical benefits when he left the financial giant under a cloud of problems.[40]

David Siegel was just one of the most recent MBA-holding hit-and-run artists to become a top US Airways executive. He joined US Airways in March of 2002 at a salary of $750,000. When he filed the company for bankruptcy in August of 2003, he conceded to a 20% pay cut to $600,000 but had already received a signing bonus equal to one full year of his original $750,000 pay. When Siegel resigned in April of 2004, employees were informed that he had received $9 million dollars in salary and stock compensation as severance from the company.

This outraged employees, but severance deals for prior US Airways executive pillagers were far worse. In February of 2003, employees were told that $35 million had been paid to three top former executives in 2002—just months before US Airways' first bankruptcy filing and after the pilots had been robbed of their wages and pensions. Captain Bob, for instance, had his salary reduced from $250,000 to $110,000 per year. Stephen Wolf, former US Airways chairman of the board, received a $15 million lump payment in March 2002. Rakesh Gangwal got a $15 million lump sum after he quit as

---

[40] See "Insiders Collected More Than $1 Billion Before Refco Collapse," *New York Times*, Oct. 20, 2005; "While Shares Fell, Viacom Paid Three $160 Million," *New York Times*, Apr. 16, 2005;"Our Opinions: CEO Rakes In Money For Nothing," *Atlanta Journal Constitution*, Apr. 4, 2005;"Take That Handshake and Shove It!: Carly Fiorina's Payoff Share Not Fair," *Pittsburgh Post Gazette*, Feb. 20, 2005; "Platinum Chutes Gives Fired CEOs a Heavenly Ride," *Chicago Tribune*, Sept. 16, 2000;"Nice Work If You Can Lose It" *The Economist*, July 14, 2005.

CEO in November 2001. Lawrence Nagin stole away with $5 million as an already retired executive vice president in March 2002. These payouts were hidden from shareholders and employees. They were deceitfully tucked deep inside a tall stack of US Airways documents filed with the court just months after the disbursements. Gangwal and Wolf were working as a team against US Airways shareholders and unionized employees—Wolf at the top of the board and Gangwal occupying the top two managerial posts.[41]

Mohnish Pabrai and Secretary Bacó discuss their talk with UPR-RP MBA students.

How Bankruptcy Builds Ivy League MBA Robber Barons

Inside corporate executives used two bankruptcy proceedings to terminate the pension plan for its unionized pilots. All told, the active and retired pilots of US Airways lost

---

[41] See "US Airways gave $35 million in pension payments to top 3 former executives", Post-Gazette, Wednesday, February 26, 2003

$1.9 billion in accrued benefits that were not funded by the plan and were not insured by the Pension Benefit Guaranty Corporation (PBGC). The PBGC is a federal agency responsible for insuring certain benefits under private defined benefit pension plans. This loss amounted to just over one-half of the $3.7 billion in total benefits that pilots had already earned as of the time the plan terminated. With US Airways' second bankruptcy, the three pension plans covering the rest of US Airways' employees were terminated and taken over by the PBGC. PBGC has estimated that the assets of these three plans cover 40% of liabilities.

The airline contended that unless it could reduce its pension expenses—what it must pay over the next seven years to cover its unfunded pension liabilities—it wouldn't have been able to obtain the federal loan guarantee and equity funding it claimed it needed to survive. The airline's executives promised pilots that they would replace the scrapped pension plan with another. They never did; they just left town.

While being cross-examined by the unionized pilots' attorney, US Airways Chief Financial Officer Neil Cohen testified that Wolf, Gangwal and Nagin received their millions in lump-sum retirement payments. The Air Line Pilots Association's spokesman Roy Freundlich said the testimony, which the union immediately posted on its website, confirmed what many pilots suspected—the airline's top executives were protecting their pensions while sacrificing those of other employees. The disclosure of the retirement payouts came at a time that saw the airline's ranks slashed by more than 16,000 and inside management wrest more than $1 billion in annual wage and benefit concessions from its unionized workers.

The pilots as a group agreed to $565 million in annual concessions without having been informed of the large executive payouts. The plan was abolished and taken over by the federal Pension Benefit Guaranty Corp. Pilots have lost their benefits in court battles. Eleven years later *The Street* reports, "*no major airline pilot group has paid a higher price than pilots from the former Crystal City, Va.-based US Airways. The pilots lost their pensions, worked for industry-low wages for a decade and suffered from a controversial seniority ruling following a 2005 merger with America West Airline.*"

Fact: *"In judging whether Corporate America is serious about reforming itself, CEO pay remains the acid test. To date, the results aren't encouraging."* — Warren Buffett in letter to Berkshire Hathaway Shareholders

PENSIONS FOR PIRATES

This wasn't the first time that Wolf and Gangwal have been criticized for their salary and benefits. In August 2001, when the deal to merge with United Airlines fell through, Wolf, Gangwal and Nagin agreed to forgo their contractual rights to resign that fall, making them eligible for severance packages totaling a combined $45 million. The three made the move amid protests from workers. In the next month, Wolf and Gangwal came under fire again from labor unions for retaining their full salaries at a time when the airline was slashing its work force and seeking concessions from its employees following the 9/11 attacks. The pair later agreed to give up their salaries and benefits for the last 15 weeks of 2001, moves that cost them nearly $200,000 apiece—a pittance compared to what they later received.

In 2000, Wolf's compensation from all sources totaled $11.6 million, including $7.6 million in reimbursement for taxes paid on restricted stock received over the years. Gangwal earned $12.1 million in total compensation, including a $7.2 million reimbursement for tax liabilities. In 1998, Wolf and Gangwal both earned nearly $35 million in salary, bonuses and stock options.

In 2004 the new CEO of US Airways, Bruce Lakefield, was awarded by the bankruptcy court a compensation package of $425,000 in annual salary and 760,000 shares of US Airways stock. By May 24, 2006, US Airways Group Inc. (LCC) traded at $43.82 per share of common stock. Lakefield's shares were worth $33,303,200. On top of that, Lakefield would get three years of base salary and bonuses if the company were sold and he lost his job. William Lauer, chairman of Allegheny Capital Management, a former US Airways investor, said, *"These payments are yet another example of outsized compensating to management that borders on looting."*

As I mentioned before, my friend Bob is a pilot for US Airways. As a Captain, his responsibilities include ensuring the safe transportation of hundreds of thousands of families to their destinations. As a Captain, he viewed his role in the corporation as a production leader, upper manager, and safety expert rather than just labor. During his career, he assumed he was adequately represented by his union, the **Air Line Pilots Association**, Int'l (ALPA). He assumed that the union was looking out for both his career and retirement, as it was supposed to, so that he could spend the majority of his efforts looking after his passengers, aircraft and crew. He strongly believed that his union was representing him fairly and in his best interest. He believed in corporate America and in what executive leadership was saying they were trying to accomplish. He saw the American Dream as something to be very proud of and he trusted the executives in charge of his company.

Sully Class Aviation

Bob started flying as a naval test pilot long before he became a commercial pilot and is known as one of the most safety conscious and competent pilots in US Airways—now American Airlines—today. The demands of the job of a commercial pilot are rigorous. This is why the job traditionally has been associated with a high salary. Pilots must spend extensive time away from home. Bob had to make a difficult decision early in his career as an airline pilot—stay in the Navy Reserves; to give up his time off each month to qualify for a government retirement or place his trust in US Airways. The carrier offered a pension that guaranteed him 50% of his highest salary over the past ten years upon retirement, which would have been half of $250,000. Bob decided that the company's pension plan would be enough to retire on comfortably. By giving up the Navy Reserves, he could spend what little time he had left with his family.

US Airways was very profitable in the 1990s amassing $2 billion in cash due to a strong economy, low fuel prices, and less restricted travel. Bob recalls:

> As the climate in the airline industry darkened starting in 2000 insiders were selling out throughout the stock market, Wolf and Gangwal needed to prop up the price so that their employee options would guarantee a vast windfall profit. They used US Airways' $2 billion in cash with a crude but effective scheme. They used the money to buy the stock back to protect their cost-free-to-them optioned equity instead of funding the employee pension. They did not save any of the cash as a safety net as the most modest of financially literate households do. They were such crappy managers they didn't even hedge the main variable cost of the firm — jet fuel —as all well

managed airlines do. Hedging was part of their train-
ing in their MBA studies—as pilots we are supposed to
know things like how to fly a plane and as MBAs they
are supposed to know things like how to hedge jet fuel!
This proved to be a very costly mistake when fuel prices
later rose. They probably estimated that they would be
retired from the company soon anyway after they exer-
cised their options. CEOs can come into a corporation,
make changes (whether good or bad) and give them-
selves in a few years a retirement plan that we all dream
of instead of 20 to 30 years of labor like everybody else.

Meanwhile Wolf and Gangwal talked extensively to the
press about a negotiated merger with United Airlines—they
talked as if the merger was guaranteed. US Airways stock
was volatile. Bob was able to swing trade his 401(k) up to
$280,000 and many other pilots were doing the same. Bob
explained:

Trap: Short selling of stock is extraordinarily risky. Jesse Livermore himself went from fortune to famine several times and died penniless on November 28, 1940 when he committed suicide. He was a major short seller in both the 1907 and 1929 stock market crashes. Lesson: Don't sell stock short!

Wolf and Gangwal didn't like the dampening affect this had on the upward run of the stock price, so they arbitrarily changed the rules of the 401(k) so that when employees traded out of the stock, they could not get back in for at least thirty days. This forced employees to buy and hold for the long term. Remember, Scott, this was a volatile airline stock, not a dividend paying utility. While we employees

were pumping money into the company, inside corpo-
rate executives were sucking it out by exercising their
inflated employee stock options. In other words, while
these US Airways corporate executives were spread-
ing a rosy picture about the stock—and its probability
of future price increases – they were selling out. The
employees were making a market for the inside corpo-
rate executives of US Airways! As insiders told the
press, the merger with United was supposed to be a sure
thing. Wolf and Gangwal bragged that sixty dollars a
share was going to be the future price for all remaining
US Airways shares. If the deal didn't go down, Wolf
would get $50 million because he had done his part of
setting US Airways up for sale.

Good ol' 'Bugsy' Siegel

Then came corporate restructurings where Wolf and Gangwal left filthy rich and brought in a hard-nosed CEO named
Siegel who was best known for his ability to break labor
unions. "What a crappy track record he had," smirked Bob.
"In just one year at the helm of Budget Rental Car, he made
enough bad business decisions to put it in bankruptcy. The
thing that 'Bugsy' (as he was known by the pilots) had going
for him was that he was friends with Wolf and had no ethics.
He made a statement at a board meeting when he arrived
that he was going to make all the corporate executive board
members millionaires and he was not going to let the pilot
pension plan get in the way.[42] Unfortunately for his rank-
and-file reputation, one of the board members was a pilot
who didn't appreciate the statement too much. Bugsy did

---

[42] Benjamin "Bugsy" Segal was a famous mafia criminal who led a giant
underground gambling operation during the Great Depression in Las
Vegas, Nevada.

the unthinkable anyway and stripped the pilots of their pensions.

"Good ol' 'Bugsy' Siegel left in just a couple of years with millions in his pocket while us pilots who had worked far harder for the firm for most of our adult lives were left behind broke." Bob is still bitter when he discusses how inside corporate executives stole everything he held dear.

Bob talked about how disappointed he was when the deal went south with the Justice Department antitrust division. "They stopped the deal! Talk about a precipitous fall in stock price," Bob lamented. "US Airways stock plummeted. 9/11 just made the slide worse."

Bob explained to me how he got started investing:

> When I got married in 1976, I purchased a house in San Diego—a little townhouse in Chula Vista—for $36,000. Two years later, I sold it for $78,000 and made $42,000. And then I went overseas, but before I did I opened a Merrill Lynch account with Johnny, the stockbroker/vice president of the firm. I made some choices and bought some stock. I bought some Occidental Petroleum that paid a huge dividend—14% back then when interest rates were through the roof. I had a couple of investments that were returning high interest rates and I felt that this was the way to go and it turned out that dividends and interest payments actually were the way to go. While I was overseas, my stockbroker called me and said, "Bob, they are about to call (retire) your shares of Occidental Petroleum so you need to buy Buttes Oil and Gas." I said, "Well, you know more than I do because you are the big stockbroker guy." So, I sold Occidental Petroleum, and guess what – they never called the stock

*like my broker said. He bought Buttes Oil and Gas for
me at $15 a share and now if you pull up the 52-week
high during that period, you never quite got to $15 per
share. However, he filled me at $15 per share. I paid $15
per share because I believe that my stockbroker screwed
me on the deal. The stock went down and down while
Occidental Petroleum went up and up. Finally, in frus-
tration, I called my broker and instructed him to sell
at $3 per share. I really lost, and today I wonder what
special incentive he got for unloading the stock on me.*

Bob discussed the dark underbelly of Wall Street—the
full-service stock brokerages. "Back in those days," he said,
"and I am sure it still goes on today, these stock brokers have
program incentives to sell certain stocks their big clients own
to get them out at a profit by selling shares to poor suck-
ers—the little guy investors—like me and you who end up
holding the bag. That was the first big negative thing that
happened to me in the stock market and is when I really lost
faith in stock brokers as being the 'all knowing stock market
go-to-guys.' I also read this book entitled the *Unemotional
Investor* that tells you more about how some of these brokerage programs work and why you should learn to hate a
full-service stock broker.[43]

That is when I went to buying and selling directly through
a Day Tech account," Bob continued. "Then they became
Ameritrade and more recently merged with TD Waterhouse
into TD Ameritrade. This freed me from the web of the
full-service broker by working strictly through an online discount trading account. There is never a reason to pay someone $200 to $500 for pushing the same button that just says

[43] Sheard, R. "The Unemotional Investor: Simple System for Beating the
Market".

buy a stock at a certain price when you can do the same for under $10!"

Bob continued with his story:

> *I came back from the Philippines where I had been stationed as a test pilot to a stateside naval aviation testing center and from there I was hired by US Airways as a commercial pilot. When I got hired by US Airways in that first year, I still had $30,000 left that I hadn't lost to my Merrill full-service broker. I got the idea that, "Hey, maybe equity options look like an interesting way to go," because I thought I could leverage myself and make all of my losses back—on calls and puts and all that. And I had a little strategy of buying a fractional out-of-the-money option on something that looked like*

Master of Ceremony Dr. Scott Brown packs up as Ismael Falcón, Mohnish Pabrai, David Rodriguez-Ortiz, and Secretary Bacó are photographed.

it would move fast and a lot in price. My first trade was in Exxon equity options. I bought forty option contracts at 35¢ apiece and sold them quickly as they increased in value to $1.25 apiece and made $4,000 right off the top. That was great! I decided I didn't know what I was doing and needed guidance.

I still had another Merrill Lynch account (because I really still hadn't learned my lesson) and my full-service broker for that account was a guy named Paul. He told me, "You have do this and you have to do that with stock options." I abandoned my plan I had developed through independent thinking (as you teach) because I thought I needed someone "educated" to give me advice as well as to share in all the fun.[44] Paul talked me into spreads and all kinds of things that just trickled away and added up to a lot — $20,000 to $30,000 lost trading options in the end. Of course, I was one of Merrill Lynch's preferred customers because I had turned over 60 trades. I felt kind of proud of that, but I eventually realized it was a marketing ploy — another psychological trap the full-service brokerages lay out for unsuspecting investors. This is how I learned that you want to trade less, not more.

Of course, I wasn't worried through all of this because I reasoned that I was fully participating in the US Airways 401(k). I figured that as long as I was putting the maximum in the 401(k) and being paid good wages as a pilot that everything would be fine. I also knew that I had an additional pilot pension plan that guaranteed me over $100,000 a year retiring at 60 — you can pretty

---

[44] Most stockbrokers do not have an education in finance—they are trained in sales!

much make it on $100,000 if you have your major debt, such as your mortgage, paid off at retirement.

I had a good trading plan. I was very in tune with airline stocks as a pilot and knew the industry like the back of my hand. Airline stocks are volatile so I would trade in and out of the 401(k) on any news of the airline that made prices jump—any time US Airways stock would make a dollar or two movement I would buy it or sell it and reverse the position when it would come back the other way. I would just be in and out in a day and knock off $2,000 or $3,000 a trade. Of course, inside corporate executives hate it when anybody else but them makes money, so they changed the rules on the US Airways 401(k). They made it so that if you sold out of the company stock in the 401(k) you had to wait 30 days to buy back in. This made you want to stay in the stock. This is when I really started to just sit in the stock. The new rule forced me to buy and hold and not sell. This really set me up for my biggest loss ever.

The stock was going up in the early and mid-1990s and then in came the big bad wolf and his teeth—Stephen Wolf as chairman and Rakesh Gangwal as CEO. Wolf was known for dressing up airlines and selling them. US Airways was still profitable and we basically came up with about $2 billion of value that the company had on the balance sheet. Of course, Wolf had options going to bed. It's funny that when you have an employee stock option plan you really have a little savings account. When we pilots are making $125,000 per year—down from $250,000 pre 9/11—or even lower-paid flight attendants, we all get maybe 7 to 10 shares of stock per year. But the executives get 200,000 to 300,000 shares a year.

What Wolf did is instead of funding our pension plan — like he was supposed to — he was buying company stock back from the market to prop up the stock price. He did this so that he could get out of his options filthy rich — and he was an employee just like us. He took the $2 billion in cash that we non-executive employees had created by doing a great job that he was supposed to be using for things like funding our retirement plans and used it to buy up the float of the stock instead. This created buying pressure that artificially inflated the stock price while Wolf and other executives sold out their employee stock options for millions before the price came crashing down.

What you see in corporate America today is that the people who do all the work — the people who are there the longest and truly make the company valuable by doing a great job day after day — get nothing in terms of meaningful employee stock options, bonuses or benefits compared to these corporate hit-and-run artists.

Executives come in, but because they have the corporate lawyers behind them fighting for their supposed "valued contribution" to the company, they get hundreds of thousands of shares of stock. They also get millions in bonuses and golden parachutes while their corporate lawyers force the company to pay the taxes. This

Trap: Most inside manipulation of stocks called "corners" in the 1800s involved the robber-barons of the time, namely, Jay Gould, Daniel Drew, Jim Fisk, Cornelius Vanderbilt and J.P. Morgan. These men "accumulated" shares from the public at low prices and later "distributed" them back to the public at high prices.

means that they get it all tax-free, and they are only an employee for two to five years until they move on to another company to strip away the employee created wealth again like financial leeches.

Also remember that these executives have control of the accounting — they have different ways to show a profit or a loss when they want. For instance, we just showed a profit in the first quarter of 2006. Yet, after all the prior doom and gloom, nobody is asking why. The reason US Airways showed a profit is that executives wanted preferential financing for the purchase of additional aircraft which will increase the value of the firm and ultimately the value of their stock options. Executives show a profit or a loss when it serves them — who knows what creative accounting goes on behind the closed doors of the inside executive-controlled boardroom.

What happened with our pensions was truly grotesque. They filed bankruptcy and then they said that our pensioned retirements were under-funded. They terminated our pilot pension plans and that got them out of millions of dollars of debt obligations as they turned it all over to the federal pension guarantee board. Then the federal pension guarantee board told the insiders to turn over their records showing that the US Airways pension fund was under-funded. The inside corporate executives of US Airways replied that they had made an accounting mistake and that it really was not under-funded but it was too late to for us to do anything about it — we got the shaft and they got the gold mine!

This is what these large U.S. corporations are doing — they are using bankruptcy to get out of their pension obligations if they can. Corporate governance has increasingly concerned itself in the United States with making a profit with less and less regard to product quality, employee family financial stability or even the good of the community. The executives constantly harp that corporations need an increased profit margin to take care of the stockholders. They find ways to pirate off all the profit from behind the scenes while they act like they are protecting the shareholders. The problem is that in the end neither the shareholders nor the employees get anything. The only winners that walk away from the board are the inside corporate executives who went to lying and cheating school.

In fact, what I have heard recently is that top places that produce these arrogantly self-interested executives — such as the Wharton School of Business at the University of Pennsylvania — have had such a problem with the bad reputation of their MBA graduates they have pumped into the market that they are now emphasizing more ethics than they used to. They are trying to employ damage control because these top schools have put out a whole generation of the most unethical, lying, cheating bastards alive on the planet. These universities also have law schools pumping out Ivy League corporate attorneys who are another big part of the inside den of thieves that know how to get around the system.

It is very frustrating and we can whine about it all we want, but the question is, "What can we do?" The good news is that you answer that question very well in this book. Now we have Doug Barker at US Airways who seems like a good CEO and seems to be doing good things, but the employees have not forgotten how they used bankruptcy to destroy our pensions and union contracts. Mr. Barker's colleagues have taken the career out of being a pilot, which is an unfortunate thing."

I asked Bob what has happened to his employer sponsored 401(k). He replied, "My 401(k) got decimated because I had it fully invested in US Airways common stock. Wolf said that the buyout was going to be at $60 per share when there was a lot of talk of a merger pre-9/11. They also expressed great confidence in the merger. When the government shot the merger down the stock dropped so fast that you couldn't get out of the way. My $280,000 turned into $14,000."

"Is that stock back up?" I asked Bob. "No," he replied, "The stock dropped to zero, they retired it and issued a new series of common stock. I lost everything." Basically, said Bob, he felt that his airline 401(k) and pension plan were both stolen by inside corporate executives.

"Executives didn't tell employees to buy stock because of the merger," he said. "But the opportunity was there. They were spreading all of this good news in the media and you could see that US Airways operations were decent."

Bob continued his discussion of the circumstances surrounding the merger and subsequent fall-out:

> *The merger with United Airways was going to be a great thing. So all of the company employees were talking about it, but the executives did nothing to explain to us the dangers of putting all of our eggs in the same basket. What is worse is when they changed the rules and you could not get back into the stock after 30 days. This made everyone afraid to get out. That tipped the balance for me because I never used to be in US Airways stock for more than a couple of days—I was in and out due to the volatile nature of the stock. But then you fall into the psychological trap of false hope and you think, "What if the stock does go to $60?" You become afraid*

of missing an opportunity. Hope and fear is what drives the whole market!

I have learned a lot from all of this and have become a competent stock investor. Things are a lot better because I buy stocks that are undervalued instead of overvalued using the knowledge that you have taught me. I also refinanced all of my debt, which you also talked me into, at low interest rates — you were a very supportive friend in that time of need. The stocks I buy today are of good companies at ridiculously cheap prices, so all I have to do is patiently wait. I am much more relaxed. I have lost my casino mentality when it comes to investing. People should not act like they are going to a casino. Just as when they walk into a Las Vegas casino thinking that they don't want to lose more than $300, but they don't set a goal about how much they want to make. Stock investing is not for entertainment, and they need to take their investing very seriously.

The vast majority of stock investors don't even do simple things like setting a profit goal — they don't know when to take a profit. I take profits now. One stock you showed me made a 100% profit and so I sold it. Now I take profits and that is really what the public needs to learn. Then I look for another undervalued stock to buy.

I also invest in ADRs outside the United States because foreign executives can't possibly be as crooked as these bastards here in the United States. Business schools in America are using this major blunder as a lesson in their courses, but we pilots are still the big losers in corporate America just because we do an honest day's work.

By giving the managers of the firm employee stock options (ESOs), they should think more like shareholders—they

Tip: Stick to an index fund if you are trading in an employer sponsored 401(k), or 403(b). I recommend the Vanguard 500 (VFINX) fund because of its large size (if available in sponsored plan menu).

should be motivated to maximize corporate performance and thus their own compensation. The problem is that an increase in the stock price of the company is not caused by management's direct actions. Internal factors, such as great employees, or external factors like increased public interest in stock investing, have as much or more to do with an increase in stock price than anything management does or doesn't do. In the 18-year bull market that ended in 2000, inside executives who reduced the operational results of the firm because of their own bad management were handsomely rewarded just because the stock rose.

Options are securities that make it possible to invest in stocks without actually owning the shares. Warrants are similar but less common. An **option** is a contract that gives one party a temporary right to buy an asset from another investor at a fixed price. Alternatively, an option can also grant the right to sell.

Options in General

Options are used in business all the time. An option to buy real estate will help you understand the way they work and lead us into a discussion of stock options. Suppose a company is interested in building a new factory and has identified a desirable site but will need six months to make a final decision on the project. How can it hold onto the right to buy the land without paying in full?

The solution is an option contract granting the firm the right to buy the land within six months at a stipulated price. That locks in the land's availability and price, but does not obligate management to not make the purchase. Of course, the company has to pay the landowner for that privilege, but this cost is a small fraction of the value of the real estate. The option is really a purchase contract that's suspended at the decision of the buyer for a limited time.

Suppose that after six months, Management decides it's not going to build the factory but notices that the price of real estate has gone up 30%. What should it do? Clearly, it should exercise its option to buy and then sell the land for a profit—all without owning the land while it appreciated. This is possible with any asset on which options are sold. Options cost less than the underlying assets, yet they confer the right to buy or sell at a locked in price. That advantage is what financial options are all about.

Stock Options

Options on stock are conceptually similar to real estate options, but they are not purchased to acquire stock. Rather, they're bought to speculate on or **hedge** against price movements that cause losses.[45] Stock options are themselves securities and can be traded in financial markets. An option to buy a stock is known as a **call option** or just a call. Options to sell tangible assets like real estate are unusual, but options to sell stock are very common. They're known as a **put option**, or just a put. I will discuss puts and calls separately in the sections that follow.

---

[45] A hedge is an investment made to reduce the risk of adverse price movements in a security by taking an offsetting position in a related security, such as a put option.

Options are the most important example of a class of financial assets known as **derivative securities**. A derivative is so named because it *"derives"* its value from the price of another *"underlying"* security, in this case the optioned shares of stock.

Investors are interested in stock options because they provide speculative leverage, a term applied to any technique that amplifies the return on an investment. Option **leverage** comes from the fact that the return on the investment in stock options can be many times larger than the return on the underlying stock just as a lever in physics increases force.

Call Options

Imagine that a stock is selling for $55 and someone offers you a contract under which he or she agrees to sell you a share for $60 anytime during the next three months. This is a basic call option. It grants you the right to buy a share at a fixed price for a specified period, typically three, six, or nine months. At the end of that time, the option expires and can no longer be exercised. **Exercising an option** is when you decide to buy (in the case of a call) or sell (in the case of a put) the underlying shares of stock according to your rights of the option contract.

The price the option holder pays for the contract is the **option price**. It's always less than the underlying stock's price. An option on a stock worth $55 giving you the right to buy at $60 might sell for $2 or $3. The stock's current price is also called the underlying price, but the $60 guaranteed price you can buy at is known as the option's **strike price, striking price,** or **exercise price**.

Ask yourself the following questions: would you pay anything for this option contract? Why? And if you would pay for the deal, what factors would make you pay more or less?

My friend Captain Bob might be willing to buy this option, because there's a chance that the stock's price will rise above $60 within the next three months. If that happens, an option owner can buy at $60 and immediately sell the shares of stock for the higher market price. For example, suppose Bob pays $1 in premium for the option. After buying the option, the stock's price goes to $63. He would exercise at the strike price of $60 and immediately sell at the underlying price of $63, making $3 cash less the $1 premium paid for the option contract—a $2 profit.

Esteemed Real Estate Attorney Nicholas Prouty is a major proponent of Puerto Rico commerce and is a local investor via Putnam Bridge. He has pledged to talk with Dr. Brown's UPR-RP MBA students.

The $2 profit is a 200% return on the $1 investment in the option. But also notice that if the stock's price doesn't rise above the $60 strike in three months, the option expires worthless and the $1 investment in premium is lost. That's a 100% loss on the investment.

Two factors make options more or less appealing. An option on a volatile stock is worth more than an option on a stock that has less **price volatility**—low volatility means that prices are not bouncing around much. This is because a volatile stock's price is more likely to go above (in the case of a call) or below (in the case of a put) the option's strike before the contract expires. **Price volatility** is how much a stock's price moves around. Measure this with **standard deviation**.

The Option Writer

There are two parties to a contract—a buyer and a seller. Don't confuse buying and selling the option contract with buying and selling the optioned stock. Until now, I have focused on option buyers who have the right to buy or sell the stock at the strike price, but what about the people who sell options?

The first person to sell an option contract is the person who creates it by agreeing to sell the stock at the strike price. He or she is said to **write an option** and is called the **option writer**.

Once the option is written, the option contract becomes a security. The writer sells it to the first option buyer who may sell the contract to someone else later on. No matter how many times the option is sold, the writer remains bound by the contract to sell to (in the case of a call) or buy (in the case of a put) the underlying stock from the current option owner at the strike price if he or she exercises. A call option writer hopes the underlying stock's price will remain stable. If it does, he or she will get to keep the option premium received from the buyer if the option contract expires worthless.

Intrinsic Value of an Option

If a stock's current price is below the strike price in the case of a call, or above the strike price in the case of a put, the option is **out of the money**. This is because the option contract buyer would not make money exercising the contract. If the stock's price is above the strike price in the case of a call, or below the strike price in the case of a put, the option is **in the money**. This is because the option contract buyer could make money exercising the contract.

When an option is in the money, it has value that doesn't depend on the stock's price moving higher in the case of a call or lower in the case of a put. This value is also called the **intrinsic value** of an option. For example, suppose the stock underlying the option is selling for $65 in the previous example. Then the option to buy at $60 must be worth at least $5, because an option owner can exercise at $60 and immediately sell the stock he or she receives at $65 for a $5 gain (less the option's price).

The option's intrinsic value is the difference between the underlying stock's price and the strike. In the case of a call, the intrinsic value is the underlying stock price less the strike. In the case of a put, it's exactly the opposite. The intrinsic value is the strike minus the underlying stock price.

Investors are willing to pay premiums in excess of the intrinsic value for stock options because of the chance that they will profit if the option goes into the money. **Option premium** is the difference between the intrinsic value of the option and the option's price. The exact amount of a particular option's premium above intrinsic value depends on the stock's volatility (**volatility premium**), the time until expiration (**time premium**), and the attitude of the market about the underlying stock—whether investors expect the market price to go up or down. The premium is generally largest when a stock is near but a little below the option's strike price—it diminishes as the stock price rises. This relationship is a result of the way option leverage changes with the price of the underlying stock.

Options and Leverage

Financial leverage is a term used to describe any technique that amplifies **return on investment (ROI)**. For example, suppose a traditional stock investment results in a 10% return. Then a leveraged investment in the same stock might result in a 40% or 50% profit in the same period. Unfortunately, leverage amplifies losses too, if the stock's return turned out to be minus 10%, the leveraged investment would have produced a 40% or 50% loss—a lot more of a thrashing than just owning the underlying stock!

Options represent one of a number of leveraging techniques in investing. Imagine that an underlying stock is trading at $58 and the premium on a call option with a $60 strike is $2. The option price is also $2 because it is out of the money and its intrinsic value is nothing. Now imagine that the stock price increases to $65, the option is exercised, and the optioned share is sold.

First let's look at an investment in the stock over the same period. It would have been purchased at $58 and sold at $65 for a $7 profit and an ROI of

$$ROI = \frac{Profit}{Investment} = \frac{\$7}{\$58} = 12.1\%$$

Now consider investing in the option. The buyer initially paid $2 for the option. Then he exercised, buying the underlying stock at $60 and immediately selling it at $65 for a $5 gain. But this profit was reduced by the $2 option price. The option buyer's net profit was $3, but since he only had the $2 option price tied up in the transaction, his ROI is:

$$ROI = \frac{Profit}{Investment} = \frac{\$3}{\$2} = 150\%$$

Notice the tremendous power of the option to multiply the investor's return. The option ROI is $\frac{150}{12.1} = 12$ *times* that of a straight stock investment! The potential for this kind of return contributes a great deal to the option's value when the stock price is just below the strike.

The call option isn't as levered when the stock is trading below the strike price. There are two reasons for that. First, the stock price has to rise higher to a make a profit on the call; secondly, the buyer has to pay for the intrinsic value and premium for the option. That makes his or her investment larger, which decreases the leverage. These factors make the time premium diminish in proportion to intrinsic value as the stock's price increases over the strike price.

Suppose the time premium is $1 when the stock's price is $65. That means an option buyer pays the intrinsic value of ($65-$60 =) $5 plus the $1 time premium, or $6 for the option. Then suppose that the stock price goes up another $7 to $72.

First, consider the return on investment in the stock. It would have been purchased at $65 and sold at $72 for a $7 profit and a return on investment (ROI) of

$$ROI = \frac{Profit}{Investment} = \frac{\$7}{\$65} = 10.8\%$$

Now consider the profit on the option. The buyer exercises at $60 and sells his share at $72 for a $12 capital gain. But the option cost \$6, so the profit on the whole transaction is (\$12-\$6) = \$6. The ROI is

$$ROI = \frac{Profit}{Investment} = \frac{\$6}{\$6} = 100\%,$$ or one-third less than the

same price movement from a lower starting point. As a result, the option is less attractive to investors and the time premium is lower. However, the out-of-the money option is riskier.

Options That Expire

It's important to keep in mind that options are exercisable only over a limited period at the end of which they expire. That makes option investing very risky. For example, if an option is purchased out of the money and never goes "into the money," it expires worthless and the buyer loses the premium paid. It's important to recognize that this is a 100% loss—options are very risky!

If a call option is purchased in the money—has initial intrinsic value—and the underlying share price goes down, then the option buyer's loss at expiration is the time premium paid less the decrease in intrinsic value. That will be a 100% loss if the stock's price drops below the strike price. As the expiration date approaches, option time premium shrinks to nill.

Trap: Options are very risky because of leverage. If you trade options, take them very seriously!

Trading in Options

Up until now, I've treated options as though buyers always hold them until they are either exercised or expire. In fact, that's not the case. An option can be bought and sold between investors at any time during the term of the normal contract. Options on selected stocks are traded on a number of exchanges throughout the country. The largest, oldest, and best known is the **Chicago Board Options Exchange**—abbreviated **CBOE**.

Price Volatility in the Options Market

Option prices move up and down with the prices of the underlying securities, but the relative movement is much greater for options. For example, an $60 strike option might sell for $2 when the underlying stock price is $58. Now suppose the stock's price goes up to $65 while there's still some time until expiration. The option sells for a price including its intrinsic value of ($65-$60) = $5 and a smaller time premium. Assume that time premium is $1. The option's price is $6—this is the intrinsic value plus the time premium.

The stock's $7 price movement from $58 to $65 is a 12.1 percent increase, but it has driven the option's price to triple its value from $2 to $6 (a 200% increase). As a result, prices in option markets are extremely volatile and fast moving.

Options Are Rarely Exercised Before Expiration

In the situation, I just described, suppose the option owner believes that further increases in the underlying stock's price are not likely—the price movement is very tranquil or dropping—and wants to close out his or her investment even though there's a good deal of time left until expiration, thus the option has lots of time premium. In that case, virtually all traders would sell the option to another investor rather than exercise it. That's because exercising brings in just five dollars, which is less than the $6 option price [($65 - $60) = $5]. Exercising means throwing away whatever value there is in time premium, in this case $1. Thus, options are rarely exercised before expiration.

The Downside and Risk

Think about the upside as well as the downside of option trading. There's a chance of a very high return through leverage, but there is also a chance of total loss. Another way of saying this is that leverage works both ways, amplifying losses as well as gains. It's a big mistake to get so caught up in the potential gains that you lose sight of the losses that are also possible. Be very cautious of option courses that promise huge yields without discussing the very real need for damage control—or the biggest payoff of all will be to the "guru" who sells you the course!

Writing Options

Investors can issue or write option contracts which are bought and sold by other investors. People write options for the premium income they receive. Option writers and buyers essentially take opposite sides of bets on which way underlying stock prices will move.

Options are written either covered or naked. With a **covered option**, the writer owns the underlying stock at the time the option is written. If the stock's price goes up and a call option buyer exercises, the writer must sell at the strike. The option writer isn't out any additional cash, but missed out on the price appreciation he or she would have had if he or she hadn't written the option.

For example, suppose Captain Bob has a share of stock purchased some time ago for $40 that's currently selling for $55. He writes a call option at a strike of $60. Suppose the stock goes to $70 and the buyer exercises. In a sense, Bob has an **"opportunity loss"** of $10 by not being able to sell the stock for a profit at $70.

Someone who writes a **naked option** doesn't actually own the underlying stock at the time he or she writes the call and therefore faces more risk. In the situation above, if the option had been written naked, the writer would have had to buy a share at $70 and then sell it at $60 to comply with the option contract, losing $10 less the option price received before. This is much riskier to the brokerage.

Put Options

A **put option** or just a put, is an option to sell at a specified price. Investors buy puts if they think the price of the underlying security is going to drop. For example, suppose a stock is currently selling for $55 and a put option is available to sell at a strike price of $50. An option buyer makes money if the stock drops to $45 buying a share at that price and selling the optioned stock to the option writer for $50. The writer is obligated to buy as per the option contract. Put options are in the money when the stock is selling below the strike price of $50 in this case.

Option Pricing Models

The price modeling problem for option values is more difficult than for stock and bond prices. It is hard to express an option's value as the present value of a stream of future cash flows. A viable option pricing model was developed in the 1970s by two well-known financial scholars,

Fact: Traditionally, the public has preferred bonds to stocks because of the more dependable interest payment. Financiers invented dividends to attract the public away from bonds.

Fisher Black and Myron Scholes.[46] The **Black-Scholes Option Pricing Model** has achieved widespread use even though it is complex mathematically. It is popular because calculators and spreadsheets can be easily programmed to carry out all the complex math from a few simple inputs. Thus, real-world practitioners use this option model most frequently.

The Black-Scholes model determines option prices as a function of a few simple variables:

1. The underlying stock price
2. The option strike price
3. The time remaining until contract expiration
4. Volatility of the market price of the underlying stock
5. The risk-free interest rate
6. Dividends

Warrants

It's important to notice that the options I have been discussing up until now are strictly bought and sold in the secondary market. That is, they're traded between investors, and the companies that issue the underlying stock the option is written on don't get involved and don't get any money when options are written or exercised.

Warrants are similar to call options but are issued by the underlying companies themselves. When a warrant is exercised, the company issues new stock in return for the exercise price. Therefore, warrants are primary market instruments. Warrants are like call options in that they give their owners

---

[46] "The Pricing of Options and Corporate Liabilities," Journal of Political Economy 81 (May -June 1973): pp. 637-654.

the right to buy stock at a designated price over a specified time period. They differ from stock options in that the firm must issue shares when a warrant is exercised.

Warrants are usually issued with other financing instruments so as to make the primary security more attractive— to sweeten it up. For example, suppose a company wants to borrow but isn't in good financial condition. Lenders (bond buyers) have rejected the corporation's bonds as junk because they have been slow at paying their debts recently. Assume the company has good long-term prospects, though, and its stock is selling for $40.

Under these conditions, lenders may be induced to buy the company's bonds if the firm attaches one or more warrants to each, giving the debt holder the right to buy a share at $50 within the next five years. The warrants provide incentives to buy the bonds if people think the stock is likely to go over $50 before five years have passed. If bond holders do exercise the warrants, then the company will receive additional cash as they issue new shares that are sold to fulfill the warrants.

Bond warrants are usually detachable and can be sold independently at a market value of their own. This effectively reduces the price of the bonds and increases their yield to the investor. Alternatively, bondholders can keep the warrants and exercise them for a quick gain if the stock's price rises above $50. Notice that if the warrants are exercised, the company receives an equity infusion based on a price of $50 rather than the higher market price. Bond prices are unaffected by the exercise of the warrants. This is not so for stock warrants.

Employee Stock Options (ESOs)

For many years, American companies have given "key" employees more stock options as part of their compensation.

Employee stock options (ESOs) are more like warrants than traded options because they don't expire for several years and strikes are set at current share prices when the options are awarded. Key employees who receive stock options get less in salary than they otherwise would—at least in theory.

Workers like being paid with options because they don't cost anything when issued. Since employees who receive options supposedly get lower salaries, promoters of ESOs pitch them as improvements to the company's financial statements by lowering payroll costs. Supporters of employee stock options argue that the practice has an important role in maintaining the United States as a leader in innovation—supporters include corporate attorneys on the payroll of inside executives. They maintain that the chance of getting rich through employee stock options attracts the best and brightest people with innovative ideas to new companies struggling to afford this kind of new talent. Corporate attorneys who profit from ESO legal fees defend their services in claiming that firms would not prosper without employee stock options. Employee stock options reduce the ownership of each of the paying shareholders in the public.

The Executive Stock Option Problem

Major recipients of the biggest employee stock option packages are senior executives. In larger companies, pay packages of top people typically include a salary in the millions of dollars and options that can generate windfall profits in the tens or hundreds of millions of dollars.

In recent years, a great deal of criticism has been directed at option-rich packages for top management. Financial economists have long argued that this kind of pay structure gives executives too much incentive to maximize stock prices. In other words, since the personal wealth of CEOs and CFOs is directly tied to stock prices through options, they may be tempted to drive prices up at the expense of investors.

To understand the danger, you must recognize that financial results from recently released SEC Form 10-Q reports move stock prices. Top executives can manipulate financial results by cooking the accounting books to increase the 10-Q report bottom-line. The situation is a classic conflict of interests in that someone is in control of the system that determines his or her own pay.

If these deceptive methods are used, earnings overstated 10-Q financial results are interpreted favorably by investors who bid stock prices up. Stocks remain overvalued until the investment community discovers what's been going on. Prices crash rapidly, destroying the savings of unsuspecting shareholders who are the real own-

Fact: The two essential characteristics of successful stock investors are *patience* and *independent* thinking!

ers. By then, high-flying inside corporate executives have exercised their options, sold the shares, and pocketed enormous sums of cash.

Company-controlled pension funds are an even more startling problem. Company-controlled retirement plans are often heavily invested in the company's own stock, the value of which evaporates when deceptive reporting is uncovered. The result is that top inside senior executives are able to effectively steal their employees retirement savings as well.

For years, the investment community wasn't overly concerned about this deception because everyone assumed auditors would keep financial results reasonably accurate.

People knew overstatements existed, but they didn't believe they were so bad. In early 2000, at the top of the biggest bull market of the last century, it became apparent that auditors couldn't always be counted on to police corporate financial reporting—they were caught up in a conflict of interest of their own. Since auditors are paid by the companies they audit, they're more likely to bow down to corrupt demands of the senior inside executives they're supposed to be watching. They interpret accounting rules liberally and sign off on financial statements that they know are likely to mislead investors.

In early 2000, the stock prices of several major corporations collapsed when the investing community learned that their financial statements contained major misrepresentations. The best-known cases were Enron, a leading player in energy, WorldCom, the telecommunications giant that owned MCI, and Tyco, a conglomerate that participates in a wide variety of businesses. In addition, Arthur Anderson, Enron's auditor and one of the world's largest accounting firms, went out of business as a result of its role in the Enron debacle. Enron employees had their retirement plans stolen from them by the inside senior corporate executives that the employees had placed their trust in. The corporate insider thieves that instigated these scandals still live in mansions.[47]

Option-based compensation wasn't the only problem uncovered. Many financial economists feel the system sets up a climate that encourages management to unduly focus on short-term financial results.

---

[47] Watch the movie "*Fun with Dick and Jane (2005)*" starring Jim Carrey and Téa Leoni. Make sure you pay close attention to the credits at the end!

The scandals led to a major review of financial reporting and auditing procedures by the accounting profession as well as congressional legislation aimed at punishing deception by senior executives. A major issue within the overhaul continues to be a requirement that companies recognize employee stock options as expenses at the time they are issued. This isn't easy to do because the same corporate senior inside executives have become so rich fleecing the public that they maintain their own special interest group to pay off congress so that such legislation is not passed. Only recently has the SEC been able to force corporations to cost employee stock options gifted to inside executives. But they still cheat by cherry-picking the inputs into the Black-Scholes option pricing model.

At present, reform is ongoing, but many issues remain unresolved. The bottom line is that senior corporate executives have power over both Washington, D.C. and the companies they rule over.

Chapter 6: Fundamental Analysis of the Stock Market

I met Hank in 2002 while I was at the University of South Carolina working on my doctorate in finance. He asked me for advice because he wasn't sure what to do with his IRA from Shell and DuPont. He told me that Merrill Lynch was courting him to manage the account for a 1% management fee. I was puzzled that such a large company would be trying to win Hank's business—they normally go after large corporate clients, and Hank was such a soft-spoken, humble man who did not strike me as rich.

CEO Nicholas Prouty of Putnam Bridge makes a point.

"How much is the IRA worth?" I asked Hank. *"1.4,"* he replied. *"Do you mean $1.4 million?"* I exclaimed with a startled look on my face. *"Yup,"* he said with a grin.

My jaw literally dropped. Hank explained that since he had retired debt-free, he didn't need the risk of the ups and downs of the stock market and had converted all of the stock into bonds—a form of fixed income investing he was less familiar with.

He told me that he had another $220,000 in the individual retirement account bringing his total stock market winnings up to $1.6 million at the age of 78 at the time. What is truly remarkable is that he never earned more than $65,000 a year and raised four sons.

When I interviewed Hank for this book, he told me he had established a stretch IRA that would not allow his children to spend the money until they were 59 ½ years old. He also said that his main "problem" was that, although he didn't need money because he was debt-free and had pension and Social Security income coming in each month, the IRS rules required that he make regular withdrawals from the IRA.

He turned down Merrill Lynch's offer to manage the account because their offices were located on the other side of the state. He didn't want to be too far from the broker-age managing his money. He decided to manage it himself with the help of an investment advisor. Hank's objective today is to extract a 6% return from the bond market using AAA corporate bonds (at the time of our interview Treasury bonds were returning about 4.5%). Hank emphasized that the secret to his success was that he believed he could succeed as a stock investor and never gave up—he stuck to his investing plan!

Here is Hank's stock market journey. He was stationed in Germany while serving in the United States Army in 1946. This was a fascinating time in history when a defeated Germany was recently divided into a capitalist west and a Marxist east political economy. The Army was hard at work acquiring as much German high technology as possible from Nazi war machine factories—like V2 rocket parts from the underground plant at Nordhausen that would lay the foundation for the American moon landing two decades later. The U.S. Army had to work fast and hard before the date of the Soviet occupation of Western Germany. Hank also witnessed the first baby steps of the rebuilding of Western Europe under the Marshal plan that would transform the area into the economic super power it is today.

Hank served his first tour of duty as a sergeant and was able to save $800 from his military income. When his tour was over, he returned to his home state of South Carolina and, under the G.I. Bill, enrolled at Clemson University—a school with an outstanding agricultural program. He graduated with a Bachelor of Science degree in agricultural economics in 1949. Shortly after graduation, Hank landed a job with the Farmers Home Administration (FHA) under the direction of the USDA. He used his savings to purchase his first car as part of his responsibilities in his first job. This was a requirement for employment with the USDA-FHA. At the time it was much more common for people not to own a car, which severely restricted mobility in the workforce.

In the USDA-FHA, Hank started in a GS-5 position with a starting salary of $3,100 per year. His supervisor talked him into putting aside $5 every paycheck to purchase U.S. Savings bonds—the most common form of investment at the time, but ultimately not the best. This humble and meager sounding first investment experience would set Hank on a path to great and enduring wealth as a stock investor—he had the wisdom to get started investing no matter how small. During the 1950s he also obtained a reserve commission to earn extra money. After 16 months with the USDA-FHA he was called to active duty in the Korean War. He served his 2 year tour as a 1st lieutenant at Ft. Jackson in Columbia, South Carolina.

Hank told me:

> *My previous experience led me to a sales career with the Shell Agricultural Chemical Division. Shell employees were encouraged to participate in Shell's Provident Fund. Saving and investing was much tougher in those days because salaries at that time started at $100 per week, and after 6 months advanced to $150 per week. The Provident Fund required an initial employee savings contribution of 2.5% of pay for 5 years matched by Shell. After 5 years, the contribution bumped up to 5% and then a few years later up again to a whopping 10% of employee salary – all fully matched by Shell. 32 years later my Provident Fund investments turned out to be a nice nest egg consisting of Shell stock and money market funds. Shell USA stock was eventually sold to Royal Dutch Petroleum for $63 per share. Royal Dutch wanted employees to get $69 per share, but surprisingly the SEC ruled against it. Royal Dutch made it up to employees later in the form of a one-time bonus — I received $34,000 because the SEC blocked the sale of my Shell USA stock at $69. This money received was additional, since they were not allowed to give us 69 dollars for our tendered stock. Can you believe that some employees did not take advantage of the Provident Fund plan?*

During employment with Shell, Hank met many colorful people common to the rough-neck petroleum industry. One such character was Bill Tuller, a Shell jobber. A jobber in the petroleum industry is a gasoline and other oil derivative products distributor, in this case a Shell products distributor. Bill told Hank that he was accumulating shares of Shell

Tip: Patience, patience, patience! Think for yourself, be patient, and don't be afraid to learn what you must learn!

Transport and Trading because they were transporters of Shell's crude oil to their refineries and even more importantly, the British part of Royal Dutch Group. Shell Transport and Trading income was the major source of finance for other Shell Companies. Hank bought as many shares of common stock in Shell Transport and Trading as he could.

Encouraged by his friend Bill to become more active in stock investing, Hank uncovered a company called Clinton Oil that was selling around $10 to $12 per share of common stock. When the stock hit $30, Hank sold it for a tidy profit—the first of many such experiences for Hank. Hank's initial success attuned him to opportunities to acquire more stock and some unusual finds popped up. For instance, the North Carolina based utility company that supplied Hank's home in South Carolina with power offered their stock thru a Customer Stock Ownership Plan (CSOP) with the common stock trading around $15 a share. He took advantage of the CSOP and ended employment with over 600 shares trading around $42-45 paying a dividend of 5.5% annually. Hank was attuned to this opportunity because Shell had a program called the Shell Employees Stock Ownership Program

(SESOP) that was then allowing him to acquire more Shell stock even faster. The SESOP was designed to allow employees to purchase additional shares above and beyond the Provident Fund—Hank jumped at the opportunity.

Later, in the mid-1980s, DuPont purchased the agricultural division of Shell. DuPont offered a similar program matching 50 cents, up to 6% of the employee's salary, for every dollar contributed. In a little more than three years he had accumulated over 1,100 shares that paid a 3.8% dividend. In summary, his participation in all of his company's plans over his working career allowed him to accumulate $1.4 million in a 33-year period. Hank's highest salary over those years was $65,000. You might be asking what Hank did with the $34,000 he was paid for his Shell USA stock. He opened an individual account that has grown to just over $200,000, bringing Hank's total stock portfolio up to a whopping $1.6 million—an extraordinary feat for a man who earned a relatively meager salary and raised 4 sons with the help of his spouse Cindy, a housewife. Today, without a financial worry in the world and living in a beautiful home in an upscale golf community in a high-class South Carolina coastal village, Cindy remembers the frustration of not having nicer cars and home furnishings that other Shell employees were buying with their *"not saved nor invested"* extra cash. None of the Shell employees who refused to participate in the company plans retired wealthy.

The main objective of **fundamental analysis** is to use fundamental factors that describe the corporation's operations and profits (or lack of profits).

These fundamental factors are obtained from the firm's accounting statements. The firm's **accounting statements** are the income statement, balance sheet, and cash flow statement. This is congruent with the 1st theory of finance by Modigliani and Miller. Managers can increase share price only by improving earnings.

THE DIVIDEND DISCOUNT MODEL

A popular model used to value common stock is the dividend discount model. The **dividend discount model (DDM)** values a share of stock as the sum of all expected future dividend payments, where the dividends are adjusted for risk and the time value of money.

Imagine a company that pays a dividend at the end of each year. Let D(t) be a dividend paid t years from now, V(0) represents the present value of future dividend streams and k is the risk adjusted discount rate. Using the dividend discount model, the present value of a share of this company's stock is measured as the sum of discounted future dividends:

$$V(0) = \frac{D(1)}{(1+k)} + \frac{D(2)}{(1+k)^2} + \frac{D(3)}{(1+k)^3} + \dots + \frac{D(t)}{(1+k)^t}$$

PRICE RATIO ANALYSIS

The **price-earnings ratio** is the current stock price divided by the annual earnings per share (EPS). This is also called the **P/E ratio.** The **earnings per share** is calculated by taking the profit during the financial year and dividing it by the average number of shares in float during the year.

The inverse of the P/E ratio is called the **earnings yield,** and is measured as the earnings per share divided by the current stock price. This is also called the **E/P ratio.** Earnings yield and price-earnings ratios are two ways to measure exactly the same thing. You will read and hear about P/E ratios a lot more than E/P ratios.

You can estimate annual EPS by multiplying the most recent earnings per share by four since earnings are reported quarterly—every three months. You get the reported value if you actually sum up the last four quarterly earnings per share values. Most analysts do it the first way, which is sloppier, but some published data sources, including the Wall Street Journal and Investor's Business Daily financial newspapers, will report to you the earnings per share using the sum of the last four quarters' figures. The difference is normally small but can be enough to confuse you.

You will read and hear a lot about growth stocks, but what does this mean? **Growth stocks** have high P/E ratios. This means that the stock has a high price relative to earnings. Here is the reasoning: if P/E ratios are measured as the current stock price over the current earnings per share, then think about two companies with the same current earnings per share. One company is a high growth company that has grown a lot in its industry or its industry has grown a lot and the company along with it. The other is a low growth company like an electrical utility company that already has all of its customers in place.

Which company would you expect to have a higher stock price, the high-growth company or the low-growth company? The high growth company, of course, should have a higher price because people think that the company will probably keep on growing. In general, companies with higher expected earnings growth will have higher P/E ratios.

Here is an example. Starbucks Corporation is a specialty coffee retailer with a history of aggressive sales growth that made stock investing Jazz musician Kenny G millions.[48] The stock trades on the NASDAQ under the ticker symbol SBUX. In early 2003, SBUX stock traded at $21.98 per share with earnings per share (EPS) of $0.57. This means that it

---

[48] Read the online article "Kenny G: Investing was crucial to my success" by CNBC reporter Jacob Pramuk.

had a P/E ratio of $\dfrac{\$21.98}{\$0.57} = 38.6$. This number is much higher than the normal stock in the S&P 500, where the 25 year P/E average is 17.78. At that time, SBUX had never paid dividends and instead had reinvested all of its earnings. In the five years prior, Starbucks had an average earnings growth of 33% per year.

It is obvious why high P/E stocks are called growth stocks, but value stocks are different. **Value stocks** are low P/E stocks. These corporations have low stock prices with high earnings. The reason some people call these stocks "value" is because they consider them "cheap" relative to current earnings.

Here is an example of a value stock. Back in early 2003, the big retailer Sears was an S&P stock trading at a price of $23.24. It had an EPS of $4.96, so the P/E ratio was $\dfrac{\$23.24}{\$4.96} = 4.7$, or about a quarter of the average S&P 500 P/E ratio of 17.78. Because of its low P/E ratio, Sears was considered a value stock at the time.

Price-Cash Flow Ratios

There is an alternative to the price-earnings (P/E) ratio called the price-cash flow ratio. A **price-cash flow (P/CF) ratio** is the current stock price divided by the firm's current annual cash flow per share. Cash flow is reported quarterly. Analysts multiply the most recent quarter times four when they calculate their ratios as before with current annual earnings. Better data sources will use the actual sum of the four quarters.

There a couple of definitions of **cash flow**, but the most common is to simply add net income and depreciation. The difference between earnings and cash flow is confusing to beginning finance students because of the way the **Financial Accounting Standards Board (FASB)** defines net income.

Basically, net income is measured as revenues minus expenses.[49] This is not logical to a finance person to whom cash is king because not all expenses are cash expenses. The most important exception is depreciation.

When a corporation buys or builds an asset they are going to use for a long time, like a new factory, FASB rules do not deduct the cost of the factory all at once—even though the factory is paid for in cash all at once. Instead, FASB directs the company accountants to deduct the cost over time. The problem is that these deductions look like cash payments, but they aren't because the actual cash payout happened when the factory was purchased. Cash flow is a lot more important than income. Here's why. Let's go back to our two company example A and B. Imagine that both companies have the same constant revenues and expenses each year for a three-year period. These constant revenues and cash expenses (excluding depreciation) give the same constant cash flows as follows:

	Company A	Company B
Revenues	5,000	5,000
Cash expenses	-3,000	-3,000
Cash flow	$2,000	$2,000

You can see that both hypothetical companies have the same $2,000 cash flow in this example. But suppose both of these companies can depreciate a $3,000 cost over a three-year period. FASB allows managers to choose different depreciation

---

[49] **Revenue** is the amount of money that a company receives from its activities, mostly from sales of products and/or services to customers. To investors, revenue is less important than profit, or income, which is the amount of money the business has earned after deducting all the business's expenses.

schedules at different times than when the expense is incurred. Let's say that A uses a straight-line while B uses an accelerated depreciation schedule; the first is spread evenly and the second is expensed more at the beginning:

	Company A Depreciation	Company B Depreciation
Year 1	$1,000	$1,500
Year 2	1,000	1,000
Year 3	1,000	500
Total:	$3,000	$3,000

Looks the same as above. But what does this do to annual cash flows and net income amounts? Remember that, for each year:

- Cash Flow = Net Income + Depreciation

you can rearrange this to:

- Net Income = Cash Flow − Depreciation

Now look what happens using this formula to calculate net income:

	Company A		Company B	
	Cash Flow	*Net Income*	*Cash Flow*	*Net Income*
Year 1	$ 2,000	$ 1,000	$ 2,000	$ 500
Year 2	2,000	1,000	2,000	1,000
Year 3	2,000	1,000	2,000	1,500
Total:	$6,000	$3,000	$6,000	$3,000

See how the two different depreciation schedules distort the net income values for each company but cash flow does not? If you didn't understand this, you would incorrectly conclude that company B is a growth company. If you did understand this you would quickly see that there is no growth in cash flow to support the growth company conclusion. Either way, this is a simple example among many that complicate fundamental analysis.

Financial analysts typically use both price-earnings and price-cash flow ratios. If a company's earnings per share is not much greater than its cash flow per share (CFPS), analysts consider this a sign of real, or quality, earnings. What they mean by "quality" is that the numbers are more likely to reflect actual cash flow—not just accounting tricks. When net earnings are higher than cash flow, this is a sign that earnings are not real.

Remember the Starbucks example with a CFPS = $1.28 and EPS = $0.57, which means it had a P/CF ratio of $\frac{\$21.98}{\$1.28}$ =17.2?

The ratio does not tell you a lot, but notice that the cash flow per share is more than double the earnings per share. This is a possible sign that earnings are not an accounting gimmick. Sears, on the other hand, had a cash flow per share (CFPS) of $2.01 and earnings per share (EPS) of $4.96. Despite the more promising looking P/CF ratio of $\frac{\$23.21}{\$2.01}$ =11.6, the fact that earnings per share are more than double cash flow per share ($4.96 versus $2.01) is a red flag that accounting gimmicks have been used to puff up profits. There are many other ways corporate executives can fake profits or losses. Be very wary of buying and selling stocks based on ratio analysis of any kind.

Price-Sales Ratios

An alternative view of a company's performance is provided by its **price-sales (P/S) ratio**. A price-sales ratio is calculated as the current price of a company's stock divided by its current annual sales revenue per share. A price-sales ratio supposedly focuses on a company's ability to generate sales growth. Essentially, a high P/S ratio would suggest high future sales growth (and thus high cash flow and high earnings), while a low P/S ratio might indicate sluggish growth.

As an example, Starbucks Corporation had sales per share of $8.73 and a P/S ratio of 2.5. Sears had sales per share of $131.30 and a P/S ratio of 0.18. There is a huge difference in P/S ratios between these two companies because they follow two very different business models. The point I want to drive home to you is that the price-sales ratio tells you a lot less than ratios based on cash flow or even net earnings. In the end only earnings increase share price.

Price-Book Ratios

Price-book (P/B) ratio is sometimes called the market-book ratio. A price-book ratio is measured as the market value of a company's outstanding common stock divided by the book value of its equity.

Book value is all the assets of the company less liabilities—everything owned less everything owed. This really makes sense to the inexperienced investor who is used to buying consumer goods off the shelf—to whom value in a piece of paper like a share of stock does not make sense. Price-book ratios attract inexperienced investors because it seems like something is being valued. The stock price is an indicator of current market value of the company in terms of its stock, so a price-book ratio simply measures what the equity is worth today relative to what it cost to create the equity. A ratio bigger than 1.0 indicates that the firm has been creating value for its stockholders, while a ratio less than 1.0 means that the company is worth less than it cost.

SERIOUS FLAWS IN THE MARKET GAUGES

There are serious problems with three of the most popular ratios that are used as individual stock gauges: dividend-price (dividend yield), price-book, and price-earnings ratios. The problem with the dividend yield ratio is that few corporations pay dividends today. A major exception are the Dow stocks, which is why a "Dogs of the Dow strategy" gave investors above average returns over a long-time horizon in the last century.[50]

Unsheltered investors don't prefer dividends which are taxed more heavily as ordinary income than long term capital gains. In other words, shareholders would rather buy low and sell high than get a large quarterly dividend.

Trap: Analyst reports are completely misleading. Analysts are forced by threat of job loss to give rosy reports about insider controlled stocks.

Bargain hunters in the stock market look for low price-book stocks that show that the company might be selling below book value. Book value is the difference between a company's assets and its liabilities expressed on a per-share basis.

Price-earnings ratios have the problem that reported earnings have been depressed by special

---

[50] Read "Beating the Dow" by Michael B. O'Higgins and there is a nifty website that runs the calculations for you every day at *www.dogsofthedow.com*

charges and should (but often aren't) adjusted for interest rates and inflation.

EARNINGS AND CASH FLOW ANALYSIS

Cash flow is a corporation's lifeblood. It will literally die without it. It is the primary source of earnings for a healthy company. It's no small wonder why analysts are obsessed with both cash flow and earnings—their goal is to predict future increases or decreases.

Sources of Financial Information

The primary source of financial information about any corporation is the **annual report to stockholders**. Most companies spend a ton of money preparing their annual report to the stockholders, and make these reports available to anyone requesting a copy. A great way to request copies of annual reports from several companies at once is to use The Wall Street Journal **annual reports service**.

Link: http://info.wsj.com/products/dswsjars.html

Beyond the direct company reports, the Security Exchange Commission also offers financial information. The SEC requires corporations that issue publicly traded securities—stocks or bonds—to prepare and submit financial statements to the commission on a regular basis. These documents are made available through the **Security and Exchange Commission Electronic Data Gathering and Retrieval (EDGAR)** archives. The **EDGAR** archives are accessible free of charge through the internet (Sec.gov).

The most important EDGAR document is the annual **10K** report, just called the "10K." Corporations have to submit an EDGAR-compatible 10K file to the SEC at the end of each **fiscal year.**[51] They are also required to file updates every quarter, called the **quarterly 10Q reports**—10Qs. The **10Q** is a mini-10K filed each quarter, except when the 10K is filed at the end of the fourth quarter. Every 10K and 10Q report contains three important financial statements: a balance sheet, an income statement and a cash flow statement. You need to understand these three financial statements.

The SEC's **Regulation FD (Fair Disclosure) Rule** says that a company has to give any short-term information to the public at the same time it provides any short-term information to analysts and stockholders who could trade in advance of the uninformed public. Most companies comply with regulation FD by distributing announcements through e-mail alerts. To get e-mail alerts automatically for stock you own or are considering buying, you only have to register at the company's website, usually in the investor relations section.

Financial Statements

Financial statements are supposed to give you the hard facts about a corporation's operating and financial performance. This is exactly why the SEC requires that public firms distribute financial statements in a timely fashion. A company's balance sheet, income statement and cash flow statements

---

[51] A **fiscal year** is a 12-month period over which a company budgets its spending, abbreviated FY. A fiscal year does not always begin in January and end in December; it may run over any period of 12 months. The fiscal year is referred to by the date in which it ends. For example, if a company's fiscal year ends October 31, 2018, then everything between November 1, 2017 and October 31, 2018 would be referred to as FY 2018. Not using the actual calendar year gives many companies an advantage, allowing them to close their books at a time that is most convenient for them.

are supposed to be essential reading for a financial analyst. Each of these statements gives a different perspective.

The **balance sheet** gives you a snapshot view of the company's assets and liabilities on a particular date. The **income statement** measures the operating performance during an accounting period, on a quarterly or annual basis, and summarizes company revenues and expenses. The **cash flow statement** reports how cash was generated and where it was used over the accounting period.

THE BALANCE SHEET

The table below shows you the year end 2017 and 2018 balance sheets for "A" corporation.

Here are a couple of things you need to know in terms of accounting language. If something is negative, like an expense or a loss, we don't use the minus symbol, but rather put it in parenthesis. In the balance sheet above, accumulated depreciation was an expense; in other words, the company seems to have paid out or lost because of this $20,000 expense in 2017. To show this is a loss, it is put in the balance sheet in parentheses like this: (20,000), which is accounting language for a negative cash flow—a loss or a cost.

Another thing to notice is that the balance sheet is broken up into sections where the bottom line of the section is the total. A main component of the balance sheet is shown by a double underline that comes from the **fundamental accounting identity** that says that assets are equal to liabilities plus equity (stock). This is how everything must "balance" out on the **balance sheet**: Assets = Liabilities + Equity. If things don't balance out when the balance sheet is prepared, accountants know that there is a mistake somewhere that has to be fixed.

"A" Corporation Balance Sheets, 2017 and 2018	Year 2017	Year 2018
Current assets		
Cash	$2,000	$1,356
Accounts receivable	1,200	1,200
Prepaid expenses	500	500
Materials and supplies	300	300
Inventory	6,000	6,000
Total current assets	10,000	9,356
Fixed assets		
Plant facilities	$35,000	$35,000
Production equipment	20,000	20,000
Administrative facilities	15,000	15,000
Patents	10,000	10,000
Accumulated depreciation	(20,000)	(17,000)
Total fixed assets	60,000	63,000
Investments		
Company B		
7% Preferred stock	$10,000	$10,000
Company C		
Common stock	10,000	
Goodwill	5,000	0
Total investments	$25,000	$10,000
Other assets	5,000	5,000
Total assets	$1,000,000	$87,356
Current liabilities		
Short-term debt	$10,000	$10,000
Accounts payable	2,000	2,000
Leasing obligations	3,000	3,000
Total current liabilities	15,000	15,000
Long-term debt	30,000	20,000
Other liabilities	5,000	5,000
Total liabilities	$50,000	$40,000
Stockholder equity		
Paid-in capital	$10,000	$10,000
Retained earnings	40,000	37,356
Total stockholder equity	$50,000	$47,356
Total liabilities and equity	$100,000	$87,356
Shares outstanding	2000	2000
Year-end stock price	$40	$36

The "A" corporation has four major asset categories: current assets, fixed assets, investments, and other assets. **Current assets** are cash or other things that will be converted to cash and used within a year. For instance, inventory will be sold, accounts receivable will be collected and materials and supplies will be used within a year.[52] Cash is the ultimate current asset. **Fixed assets** have an expected life of more than a year and are used in normal business operations for things like manufacturing equipment, real estate and furniture. Fixed assets may be tangible or intangible. Property, plant and equipment are the most common **tangible fixed assets** while rights, patents and licenses are common **intangible fixed assets**. Except for land, all fixed assets depreciate in value over time—as does your car. Investments include various securities held for investment purposes. **Goodwill** measures the premium paid over market value to acquire an asset. For instance, a company may pay $50 per share for a stock with a market price of $40 per share when acquiring a very large block of stock. Other assets include miscellaneous items that don't fit into any of the other asset categories. The sum of these four categories of assets is the firm's **total assets**.

The "A" company balance sheet has three major liability categories: current liabilities, long-term debt and other liabilities. **Current liabilities** have to be paid within a year. Examples are **accounts payable** and accrued taxes. **Long-term debt** includes notes, bonds or other loans with a maturity longer than one year. Other liabilities include miscellaneous items not belonging to any other liability category.

---

[52] **Accounts receivable** is money that is owed to a company by a customer for products and services provided on credit. A specific sale is generally only treated as an account receivable after the customer is sent an invoice.

Stockholder **equity** is the difference between total assets and total liabilities. This includes **paid-in capital**, which is the amount received by the company from issuing common stock in the case of an initial public or seasoned offering, and retained earnings. Retained earnings is defined as slack cash when not paid out as dividends. It should be used to finance company growth, but slack often pays for executive lifestyle excesses.

Financial analysts like to use a **condensed form** that reduces the full balance sheet to a summary. This simplifies analysis while revealing the basic structure of the company's reported assets and liabilities. The analyst has to decide how much to simplify. The table below shows a **condensed balance sheet** for the "A" company.

"A" Corporation Condensed 2017 Balance Sheet			
Cash	$2,000	Current Liabilities	$15,000
Operating Assets	8,000	Long-term Debt	30,000
Fixed Assets	60,000	Other Liabilities	5,000
Investments	25,000		
Other Assets	5,000	Stockholder Equity	50,000
Total Assets	$100,000	Total liabilities and Equity	$100,000

Notice that current asset rows are reduced to two components, cash and operating assets. Cash is separated from operating assets for a good reason—net cash increases from the cash flow statement are used to adjust cash on the balance sheet. This is more clearly shown to you by first separating current assets into cash and operating assets.

The Income Statement

The table below is a **condensed income statement** for the "A" Corporation.

"A" Corporation Condensed 2018 Income Statement	
Net sales	$ 90,000
Cost of goods sold	$ (70,000)
Gross profit	$ 20,000
Operating expenses	$ (13,000)
Operating income	$ 7,000
Investment income	$ 700
Interest expense	$ (2,000)
Pre-tax income	$ 5,700
Income taxes	$ (2,056)
Net income	$ 3,644
Dividends	$ (1,000)
Retained earnings	$ 2,644

This income statement reports revenues and expenses for the corporation over a one-year accounting period. Look at it carefully and make sure you get familiar with its top-down structure to the all-important "bottom line".

The income statement begins with net sales, from which **cost of goods sold (COGS)** is subtracted to yield gross profit. Cost of goods sold vary directly with the level of production and sales. Next, operating expenses are subtracted from gross profit to give **operating income**. Operating expenses are indirect costs of administration and marketing—costs that do not vary directly with production and sales.

In addition to operating income from its own business operations, the "A" company has investment income from preferred stock dividends. Publicly traded corporations buy interests in other companies usually through preferred stock, as opposed to common stock, due to tax benefits described below. Adding this investment income and then subtracting interest expense on debt yields pre-tax income. Finally, subtracting income taxes from pre-tax income gives net income. You will read and hear about the "**bottom line**" – this is net income, because it is the last line of the income statement. To simplify this example, I have added dividends and retained earnings information that are items that often appear in a separate financial statement. Net income is the sum of dividends and retained earnings: Net Income = Dividends + Retained Earnings.

The Internal Revenue Service (IRS) of the U.S. federal government permits a company to exclude 80% of the dividends received from another company from federal income tax. This means only 20% of the preferred stock dividends that the company received from company "B" (look at the balance sheet) are taxable. For example, "A" corporation receives $700 in dividends from "B" company, but only has to pay taxes on $140 (20% of $700). The normal corporate tax rate is 40%, so in this example the actual tax amount is $56 (40% of $140).

The Cash Flow Statement

The **cash flow statement** is specific to finance because it shows where a company generated cash and where cash was used over a specific accounting period—something not particularly interesting to accountants, yet vital to financial managers. The cash flow statement puts all cash flows into one of three categories: operating cash flows, investment cash flows, and financing cash flows.

The table below shows a condensed cash flow statement for the "A" corporation.

"A" Corporation Condensed 2018 Cash Flow Statement	
Net income	$ 3,644
Depreciation	$ 3,000
Operating cash flow	$ 6,644
Investment cash flow [a]	$ (15,000)
Financing cash flow [b]	$ 9,000
Net cash increase	$ 644

[a] December 2017 purchase of 50% interest in B company for $15,000 (including $5,000 goodwill).
[b] Issue of $10,000 par value 8% coupon bonds, less a $1,000 dividend payout.

The cash flow statement begins with net income, which is the main accounting measure of earnings for a corporation. Net income and cash flow, however, are not the same and are often very different in magnitude. The main reason for the difference is because income has **non-cash items**. Depreciation is a non-cash expense that must be added to net income when cash flows are calculated. Adjusting net income for non-cash items gives **operating cash flow**.

Operating cash flow is the first of three cash flow categories in the cash flow statement. The second and third categories are investment cash flow and financing cash flow. **Investment cash flow** (or "investing" cash flow) includes any purchases or sales of fixed assets and investments. For example, "A" corporation's purchase of "B" company preferred stock reported in footnote 'a' is an investment cash flow. **Financing cash flow** includes any funds raised by an issuance of securities or expended by a repurchase of outstanding securities. In my example above, the "A" corporation's $10,000 debt issue and $1,000 preferred dividend payout reported in footnote 'b' are examples of financing cash flows.

Standard accounting practice instructs that dividend payments to stockholders are financing cash flows—interest payments to bondholders are operating cash flows. The main reason for this is that dividend payments are discretionary. The managing directors have the discretion to decide whether to pay dividends, but interest payments are mandatory and must be paid to bondholders. Also, interest payments are tax-deductible expenses, but dividend payouts are not tax-deductible. In any case, interest payments are cash expenses reported on the income statement. Since they are cash expenses, they do not appear in the cash flow statement to reconcile the difference between income and cash flow.

The sum of operating cash flow, investment cash flow, and financing cash flow yields the net change in the corporation's cash. This change is the bottom line of the cash flow statement and reveals how much cash flowed into or out of the company's cash account during an accounting period.

Performance Ratios and Price Ratios

Annual reports to stockholders and SEC 10Ks have various items of supplemental information about the company. For example, certain profitability ratios may be reported to help analysts understand the company's operating efficiency. For the "A" corporation, I calculate some standard profitability ratios in the table below using data from hypothetical statements above.

Ratio	Formula	Calculation
Gross Margin	$\dfrac{Gross\ profit}{Net\ sales}$	$\left(\dfrac{\$20,000}{\$90,000}\right)(100) = 22.22\%$
Operating margin	$\dfrac{Operating\ income}{Net\ sales}$	$\left(\dfrac{\$7,000}{\$90,000}\right)(100) = 7.78\%$
Return on assets (ROA)	$\dfrac{Net\ income}{Total\ assets}$	$\left(\dfrac{\$3,644}{\$100,000}\right)(100) = 3.64\%$
Return on equity (ROE)	$\dfrac{Net\ income}{Stockholders\ equity}$	$\left(\dfrac{\$3,644}{\$50,000}\right)(100) = 7.29\%$

Notice that you have to multiply by 100 to express a ratio in percentage terms. This is normally what you will read in analyst reports and in the financial newspapers. Notice that **return on assets (ROA)** and **return on equity (ROE)** are calculated using current year-end values for total assets and stockholders equity. You could argue that it makes just as much sense to use prior year values for these calculations, but current year-end values are what everyone uses.

Annual stockholder reports and SEC 10Ks may also report per-share calculations of book value, earnings and operating cash flow, respectively. Per-share calculations require the number of common stock shares outstanding. For instance, "A" corporation's balance sheet reports 2,000 shares of common stock outstanding. I've used this to calculate per-share values as follows:

Ratio	Formula	Calculation
Book value per share (BVPS)	$\dfrac{Stockholder\ equity}{Shares\ outstanding}$	$\left(\dfrac{\$50,000}{2,000}\right) = \$25$
Earnings per share (EPS)	$\dfrac{Net\ income}{Shares\ outstanding}$	$\left(\dfrac{\$3,644}{2,000}\right) = \$1.82$
Cash flow per share (CFPS)	$\dfrac{Operating\ cash\ flow}{Shares\ outstanding}$	$\left(\dfrac{\$6,644}{2,000}\right) = \$3.32$

It is important for you to notice that I calculate the cash flow per share (CFPS) using operating cash flow, not the bottom line on the cash flow statement. When you hear the words "cash flow" in corporate finance, this is operating cash flow.

Remember the price ratios I taught you earlier? You can use the per-share values above and "A" corporation's year-end price of $40 per share to get the following rounded price ratios:

Ratio	Formula	Calculation
Price-book (P/B)	$\dfrac{Stock\ price}{BVPS}$	$\left(\dfrac{\$40}{\$25}\right) = 1.6$
Price-earning (P/E)	$\dfrac{Stock\ price}{EPS}$	$\left(\dfrac{\$40}{\$1.82}\right) = 22$
Price-cash flow (P/CF)	$\dfrac{Stock\ price}{CFPS}$	$\left(\dfrac{\$40}{\$3.32}\right) = 12$

PRO FORMA FINANCIAL STATEMENTS

Pro forma financial statements show the forecasted (projected) operating results of possible future changes in the income and cash flow statement as well as the balance sheet. You will see three of these: pro forma income statements, pro forma balance sheets and the pro forma cash flow statement.

Chapter 7: Technical Analysis of the Stock Market

Lan Turner decided in the early '90s to create a trading simulator on the computer that has won accolades worldwide. We became friends during my Ph.D. studies. His company gifted me part of the data I used for my University of South Carolina doctoral dissertation in finance on slippage sponsored by the Chicago Board of Trade (CBOT). He recounts:

> *One of the largest losses I ever had was from a tip I received off the television. These guys had an expert on the TV and he was talking about how great this stock was going to be and how wonderful it was. I believed him—fell into the trap—and threw a chunk of money in there. Three months later, I had half of what I had in there. This was one of the things that opened my eyes to the danger of taking tips off of the TV. Like they say on Wall Street, "If you are hearing it on the news it's already too late, because everybody else in the market that creates the news has already taken advantage of it." That is why I ignore the news and turn to technical analysis to guide my investing.*
>
> *I also started to wonder if there was a way to practice in the markets without risking. I thought of the naval flight simulator, which is really just a piece of software, and decided that there must be a way to create simulation software for investors. Then I became a futures trader and really became motivated to find a way to practice*

*risk-free. If I had our simulator back then, I would never
have made some of my worst errors as an investor.*

*When I started investing, I knew absolutely nothing!
One of my biggest mistakes when I first started trading
was that I didn't even know how much I had invested
or even how much I was risking. I didn't know where
the decimal point went. I had the decimal point in the
wrong spot. I thought I was investing $100 and I was
really investing $1,000 because I had the decimal point
in the wrong spot. Questions like, "Hey, where does
the decimal point go?" sounded to me like too dumb of
a question to ask. So I made the mistake. It is like Dr.
Brown says all the time, because he started from scratch,
too: "There are no dumb questions!" You can't ask a
dumb question in this industry, because if it is a question that you might have and not having the answer is
risking your money. When your money is on the line
– well then, man, you have to ask that question and
someone has to answer it for you—hopefully the right
someone. You have to be able to find that answer. We
can't be untouchable and people have to be comfortable
asking these questions. The great thing about both our
organizations—Gecko Software and Dr. Scott Brown—
is that if you are reading this, you can enroll and ask
us in a "There Are No Dumb Questions" community
of successful investors that started right where you are
today.*

*We have been working very closely with Dr. Brown to
bring out the new version of our simulator. We have for
the last eight years been working very diligently over
in the futures industry, which is the background that
I come from. Because of the success of our simulator
over there, we have received a number of awards in the*

CEO Nicholas Prouty of Putnam Bridge listens to discussion of his point by Secretary Bacó and CEO Richard Carrión.

industry and our clients have asked us to bring the simulator into stocks. And we have done that. This is very important, because now you can practice what Scott teaches and get years of experience with no risk! Also, once you become an independent and unique thinker, as Scott wants you to be, you will probably come up with investing ideas of your own. This is also very important, because now you can trade those ideas in the stock market without risking any of your money and decide for yourself if they are worth pursuing. The comment we hear the most from our clients is that our investing simulator radically reduces their anxiety about investing in the markets because they can "fly the jet before they are on the hot stick" for less than $100 a month.

You can get his free course at http://worryfreewealth. com/offers/, train in it, and go back and practice in

Track n Trade High Finance, *because it is an investing simulation program. You can go back and simulate investing forward from any point in time and actually test your skills to see if what you think is going to happen will happen in the market. It also has the ability to track intra-day data. Our simulator is also the best way to gain experience as a technical investor, but also helps fundamental investors.*

Tip: The trend is your friend!

There is a completely different framework than fundamental stock market analysis. This approach is called **technical analysis**, and it focuses on three types of information exclusively: (1) historical price movements, (2) trading volume, and (3) investor psychology. Technical analysis techniques are centuries old, dating back at least to samurai-dominated imperial Japan, where merchants traded rice using these techniques. These downtrodden managers drove their oppressors into financial ruin, collapsing the Japanese samurai system.

Investors with a positive market outlook are called "bulls." A rising market is called a **bull market**. On the other side, pessimistic investors are called "bears" and a falling market is called a **bear market**. Technical analysts hunt for bullish or bearish technical signals about the direction of the general market and specific stocks.

DOW THEORY

Dow Theory was invented in the late 1800s and is considered the birth of technical analysis. It is named for **Charles**

Dow, co-founder of the **Dow Jones Company** and an editor of its newspaper *The Wall Street Journal*. The main point of Dow Theory is that there are three forces continually at work in the stock market: (1) a **primary market trend**,[53] (2) a **secondary reaction** or **secondary market trend**, and (3) **daily fluctuations**. The primary market trend is either bullish (up) or bearish (down). It reflects the long-run direction of the market.

For limited periods of time, the market can depart from its primary direction. These departures are called secondary reactions, or secondary market trends, and may last for weeks—up to six months. A general market trend is eliminated by a market correction, which is a reversal in the primary market direction (trend). Daily fluctuations are essentially noise and are of no real importance. The basic purpose of the Dow Theory is to signal changes in the direction of the primary trend. This is monitored by two stock market indexes, the Dow Jones Industrial Average (DJIA) and the Dow Jones Transportation Average (DJTA). If one of these indexes breaks the primary trend but the other does not, then this is viewed as a secondary market trend. If both break the primary trend, then this is called a **confirmation** that the market has shifted from a bull to a bear market or vice-versa per Dow theory.

Support and Resistance Levels

A key concept in technical analysis is support and resistance. A **support level** is a price below which a stock or a market index is unlikely to fall. A **resistance level** is a price above which a stock or the market acts like it can't rise above.

---

[53] Market trend is the slope of the share price over time.

As a stock's price (or market index) falls, people reduce selling (as compared to buying) and at some point, the downtrend bottoms out as bargain hunters start buying again. The new buying activity supports the stock price above a level visible on a price chart. A resistance level occurs for exactly the opposite reasons. The price rises. More people buy the stock (as compared to people selling) and it goes up in price. As the price goes higher, more people who have bought at lower prices start selling to take a short-term profit. The stock reaches a point where it "tops out" and falls back.

Technical analysts view resistance and support levels as psychological barriers because stocks seem to take a while to hit a level and then move up (or down) fast once they break through. For instance, as the DJIA approaches levels with many zeros—like 10,000—you will read and hear of "psychologically important" barriers in the financial press. A **breakout** occurs when a stock or a market index passes through a support or resistance level. A breakout usually continues up or down for a while after it occurs. Not only is technical analysis a potentially profitable way to analyze the stock market, but it is also a lot of fun and has lots of colorful language.

TECHNICAL INDICATORS

Technical analysts forecast the direction of the market in not only stocks but also futures and Forex. I will discuss technical indicators specifically used for the stock market first, then give you a sense of other indicators that you can use.

MARKET BREADTH

The idea behind market breadth is to attempt to measure the overall health of the stock market, working down through sectors to individual stocks. Your objective is to pick stocks in the best groups in market conditions when the stock market is healthy in terms of technical indicators. You can measure market breadth using advancing versus declining issues, new highs versus lows, and up volume versus down volume.

THE ADVANCE-DECLINE LINE

This is the most commonly used measure of market breadth. Every day on any stock exchange there are issues that advance (increase in share price), decline (decrease in share price), or do not change in price at all. The way the **advance-decline (AD)** line is calculated is by simply subtracting the number of declining issues from the number of advancing issues.

If there are more advances than declines, the number is positive. If there are more declines than advances, the number

CEO Nicholas Prouty of Putnam Bridge, CEO Richard Carrión of Banco Popular, and Secretary Bacó of the Puerto Rico Department of Commerce and Economic Development pose for a photo after their panel discussion of the Puerto Rico real estate market.

is negative. The day's number is added to the cumulative AD line to display the trend. The basic idea is to make sure that the AD line and the market averages are trending in the same direction (don't diverge).

The McClellan Oscillator is constructed by taking the difference between two exponential moving averages of the daily NYSE advance-decline values. Specifically, the **McClellan Oscillator** is the difference between the 19-day (10%) trend and the 39-day (5%) trend.

New Highs Versus New Lows

To measure market breadth, you need to know the number of stocks hitting new 52-week (yearly) highs or new 52-week lows in a chart of **new highs versus new lows**. Since the daily values are erratic, these technical charts are smoothed with a ten-day moving average.

Upside Versus Downside Volume

This is the third and final piece of data you need to measure the breadth of the market. **Upside volume** is the trading volume of advancing shares, **while downside volume** is the trading volume of declining shares.

The Arms Index

The **Arms Index**, named for its creator Richard Arms, is a ratio of a ratio. A ratio is just a fraction. The numerator—the top part of the fraction—in this case is the ratio of the number of advancing issues divided by the number of declining issues. The denominator is the advancing volume divided by declining volume. The purpose of the Arms Index is to gauge whether there is more volume in rising or falling stocks. A reading below 1.0 tells you that there is more volume in rising stocks and a reading above 1.0 says that there is more volume in falling stocks. On an intraday basis for day traders, a very high Arms Index reading is bullish, and a very low reading is bearish. The Arms Index is a contrarian indicator that trends in the opposite direction of the market that can be used for intraday trading by tracking its direction and for spotting signs of short-term market extremes.

CHART CONSTRUCTION

The daily bar chart is the most commonly used chart in technical analysis, but there are also line charts, point and figure charts, and candlestick charts.

Arithmetic versus Logarithmic Scale

The vertical price shows an equal distance for each unit of change on the **arithmetic scale**. Price distance is unequal for each unit of change on the **log scale**.

Intraday Charts

The **intra-day chart** shows you one day's session of price activity, where each blip is a transaction. These charts give you a sense of the size and movement of the bid-ask spread during the day. They are very useful when you are trading in an illiquid stock. *Intra* is a Latin word that means inside. Since this chart is intended to show activity within one day it is called an "intra" day chart.

Trap: Con artists target people in cities and small communities with Ponzi scheme high-yield investment programs. Once they take your money, they leave your legal jurisdiction and there is not a thing you can do about it. If it sounds too good to be true or if you don't understand some high-yield investment program just say *"no."*

Inter means "between" in Latin. These are the three **inter-day charts**.

Daily Charts

The **daily chart** condenses an entire day's price activity into one bar that shows the open, high, low and close prices during the day. Normally, daily charts will show a year of trading.

Weekly and Monthly Bar Charts

The **weekly chart** shows you an entire week of price activity in each bar. The **monthly chart** shows you an entire month's price activity.

TREND

The **trend** is simply the recent direction of the market. An **uptrend** is a series of successively higher price peaks. A **downtrend** is just the opposite—a series of declining peaks and troughs. Horizontal peaks and troughs, on the other hand, are a **sideways trend** known as a **price channel** or a **trading range**.

The trend has three classifications—**major trend, intermediate trend** and **near-term trends**. There is not a lot of consensus as to exactly how long each is, but here is a rule of thumb. Dow Theory says that a major trend has to be in effect at least a year to be confirmed. The intermediate trend is three weeks to less than a year. The near-term trend is price movement in the same direction for two to three weeks.

After the violation of a new up trend line, the stock price will often decline a bit before rallying back to the bottom of the old uptrend line (now a resistance line). **Fan lines** can be drawn along successive peaks to help you deal with minor trend breaks, where you can buy more or place a **stop-loss order.**[54]

REVERSAL PATTERNS

There are two major categories of price patterns—reversal and continuation. **Reversal patterns** imply that an important reversal in trend may be taking place. The **continuation pattern**, on the other hand, tells you that the market is only pausing for a while, possibly to correct for a near-term **overbought** or **oversold** market condition, after which the existing trend should resume. It is very important for you to learn to recognize between these two types of patterns as early as possible during a reversal so that you can take appropriate action.

The Head and Shoulders Reversal Pattern

In the case of the **head and shoulders reversal top pattern**, there is a major uptrend in which a series of rising peaks and troughs gradually begin to lose momentum. This is bearish. With this pattern you want to watch the **neckline** for a break. The neckline is projected across the top of the shoulders of a bullish head and shoulders pattern or the bottom of the shoulders of a bearish head and shoulders pattern. The **head and shoulders reversal bottom pattern** is just the opposite and is a bearish pattern.

Saucer Bottom Reversal Pattern

Saucer bottoms are usually spotted on weekly or monthly charts that span several years. The longer the saucer bottom lasts, the larger the rise.

---

[54] A stop-loss order is an order to sell (buy) when the price of a stock falls (rises) to a designated level.

CONTINUATION PATTERNS

Triangles

There are three types of triangles. The **symmetrical triangle** shows up as converging trend lines like a sideways pyramid. This is also called a **coil**—because the stock price is "coiling up" for a break-out—and breakouts from these patterns are spectacular. The **ascending triangle** has a rising lower line with a flat or horizontal upper line. The **descending triangle** is just the opposite of the ascending triangle. These are also called **wedges**.

Flags and Pennants

The **flag** and **pennant** are brief pauses in upward or downward market moves.

VOLUME

Volume is the total amount of trading activity on an exchange or in a single stock for that day. Volume is plotted on daily, weekly and monthly charts. Volume is a major clue as to when stocks are primed to rise and during **blow-off tops** when insiders are selling out of a stock.

LONG-TERM CHARTS

Long-range charts of five years or more provide a perspective on the market trend that is impossible to see with daily charts alone. One of the greatest advantages of technical analysis is its application over virtually any time dimension easily. Contrary to popular opinion, longer-range forecasting is best done with technical, not fundamental analysis. Trend analysis, support and resistance levels, trend lines, percentage retracements, and price patterns all lend themselves very well to the analysis of long-range price movements. If you do not consult long-range price charts, you will miss an enormous amount of valuable price information absent from financial reports regarding momentum and price impact. Momentum is trend. Price impact is the interaction between trading volume and trend.

MOVING AVERAGES

The moving average is one of the most versatile and widely used of all technical indicators. The **moving average** is a device to identify or signal that a new trend has begun or that an old trend has ended or reversed by averaging the price data.

OSCILLATORS

The **oscillator** is extremely useful in non-trending markets where prices fluctuate in a trading range horizontally—it is very useful in flat-trending markets. Short-term stock traders, called **swing traders** or **market timers**, use oscillators to try to profit from flat, trendless sideways markets. The oscillator identifies overbought or oversold conditions in the price channel. The idea is that if the market is overbought— at the top of the channel—that it will soon begin to fall back to the bottom of the channel from selling pressure. At the bottom of the channel, the oscillator is designed to tell you if the market is oversold, and may soon rise to the top of the channel from buying pressure.

Momentum is the most basic of all oscillators and is positive or negative around a zero line. The formula for momentum is $M = P_0 - P_i$ where P_0 is the latest closing price and P_i is the closing price i days ago. 10 days ago, is the most common lag time. Momentum exists in all time frames from the high-frequency tick through the low-frequency monthly chart. A relative strength index when compared against all other stocks in the market is a useful gauge of the strength of momentum.

A **relative strength index** is calculated on an index as follows:

$$RSI = 100 - \frac{100}{1 + RS} \quad where \; RS = \frac{Average \; of \; x \; days' \; up \; closes}{Average \; of \; x \; days' \; down \; closes}$$

The **stochastic (K%D) oscillator** is based on the occasional tendency for up-trending prices to have daily closing prices that tend to be closer to the upper end of the intraday price range. Conversely, in downtrends, the closing prices are near the lower end of the intraday range. The idea is to figure out where the most recent closing prices are in relation to each intraday price range over a desired time period. The K line is:

$$\%K = 100 \left[\frac{(C - L14)}{(H14 - L14)} \right]$$ where C is the latest close, L14 is the lowest low for the last 14 periods, and H14 is the highest high for the same 14 periods (a period can be a day, a week, or a month). The %D line is a 3 period moving average of the %K line.

Larry William's %R is based on a similar concept of measuring the latest close in relation to its price range over a period. Today's close is subtracted from the price high of the range. The difference is divided by the total range for the same period.

Moving Average Convergence/ Divergence (MACD) is the difference between two exponentially smoothed moving averages of closing prices (default is the last 12 and 26 days or weeks). The slower line (called the signal line) is by default a 9 period exponentially smoothed average of the MACD line. The actual buy and sell signals are given when the two lines cross.

POINT AND FIGURE CHARTING

In the 1880s and 1890s, this was known as the "book method" of charting. The **point and figure chart** is a study of pure intraday price movement used most often by day traders. The *x* columns represent rising prices and the *o* columns represent falling prices. Each time a column of x's moves one box above a previous column of x's, an upside breakout occurs. Alternatively, when a column of o's declines one box under a previous column of o's, a downside breakout occurs.

JAPANESE CANDLESTICKS

Charting market data in **Japanese candlesticks** uses the same data available for standard bar charts. This charting method uses open, high, low and close prices, but in a much more visually appealing form. Different body and shadow combinations have different meanings. Days in which the difference is great between the open and close prices are called long days. Days in which the difference between the open and close price is small are called short days. These charts can also be shown in daily, weekly or monthly form.

ELLIOT WAVE THEORY

Elliot Wave Theory compliments Dow Theory. There are three important aspects of wave theory: pattern, ratio and time. The **Fibonacci number sequence** forms the mathematical basis for the Elliot Wave Theory. Part of the Fibonacci number sequence is as follows: 1, 2, 3, 5, 8, 13, 21, 34, 55, 89, 144, etc. See the pattern? One of the most important Fibonacci rules is that corrections take place in five waves.

TIME CYCLES

People have noticed – what at least appear to be – **time cycles** in the natural world. Atlantic salmon peak in abundance on average every 9.6 years, 22.2 years pass between international battles, sunspot activity increases every 11.1 years, the real estate market goes boom to bust every 18.3 years, and 9.2 years pass between bull market tops in the stock market. Analysts measure cycle lengths from high to low. The three qualities of cycle are amplitude, period and phase.

Chapter 8:   The Strong Forces and Players Behind the Market!

Head of media relations for the Puerto Rico Department of Commerce and Economic Development Patricia de la Torre de Haro (along with Annie Mustafa, MBA) are important master-mind friends of Dr. Brown greatly assisting in the education of UPR-RP MBA students.

Fred left a job with John Deere in the agricultural industry to become a university business professor. The three cash flow centers of a university are the medical school, law school and MBA programs. For this reason, those of us academically qualified Ph.D.-holding business professors are very highly paid. Fred did several smart things. The first was to take full advantage of the university 403(b) plan. The second was to use his good credit and high income to purchase a home in the most desirable part of town. As a friend, he approached me seeking advice because he wanted to get his savings earning more than just bank interest.

He had purchased a large piece of land for $75,000 in his home state and wanted to build and retire to a dream home. Throughout his working life, Fred had methodically saved and bought his way into a lot of net worth. He had $200,000 in home equity, $200,000 in his 403(b) and $50,000 in savings. He would also have $2,300 per month coming in from Social Security and a $400 pension from his employer prior to obtaining a Ph.D. and becoming a professor. His wife would also have Social Security coming in.

I told Fred to work the numbers backwards to figure out how much he should invest in the stock market. My first big concern was that, upon retirement, Fred would lose his health insurance plan from the university. Fred told me that he wasn't worried, because both he and his wife had "good genes." I explained that 87% of all bankruptcy cases are from three reasons: job loss, divorce and illness. After listening to me, he realized that he could use the small pension to pay for a good health plan, and I congratulated him wholeheartedly on the decision.

The next step Fred had to take was to work out the budget for building his dream retirement house in his home state. I told him to ask the realtor who had helped him purchase the land to give him the range of costs per square foot for new home construction. I explained how important it was to take the high estimate and then add an additional 30% for unexpected costs and furnishings. When, I told him to be most concerned about working out a building budget that would make sure he would be debt free after selling his current residence and moving to his dream home he laughed and said, *"It's great to finally hear someone who speaks my language!"* He could then invest a fraction of what he had left over, putting the bulk into treasury bills for emergency savings.

Fact: Wall Street works hard to make stock investing seem harder than it is. The last thing the equities industry wants is retail investors who think on their own.

My trading system is based on evidence of price impact patterns that form as smart investors are buying low and selling stock at historic high prices to **dumb investors.** Price impact is the interaction between trading volume and price trend. Retail stock investors are attracted into the market hoping for a quick profit from hype at the top of a bull market. In 1999 and 2000, the majority of insiders were dumping their stock holdings on the public. And the public was buying it up as fast as they could dump it.

Once the market crashes, as it did from 2000 to 2003, inexperienced investors become discouraged and begin selling out at historic low prices. Investors buying stock at historic prices are of two classes. The first group of bottom buyers is composed of highly **experienced investors** who are astute as to the cyclic rise and fall of the general stock market and individual stocks. The second group consists of insiders who must report all of their stock purchases and sales to the SEC. If an individual owns 5% or more of the float of a stock or is a manager or director, then they are in this reporting class of **insiders**. Pay attention to the gifting and selling of ESOs by the top inside executives—the CEO, CFO, COO, chairman of the board and president. Anecdotal evidence and recent SEC prosecutions of smaller boiler room "pump and dump" schemes reveals that hidden insiders still manipulate penny stocks—watch the movie *Boiler Room* with Ben Affleck.

Practitioners of value investing include Warren Buffett.[55] Value investing normally utilizes such valuation measures as price-to-book ratio, price/earnings ratio and yield, but earnings are an imperfect guide. By combining long-term technical charts and looking for well managed companies, I look for **long-term price impact**.

Price impact investing involves studying long-term daily, weekly and monthly charts to look for price and volume patterns that discourage the public out of buying low priced shares of stock. Meanwhile experienced investors buy and hold for the rise.

INEXPERIENCED PUBLIC INVESTORS

What happens when large groups of individuals in the public who know absolutely nothing about the stock market come and go en masse? The answer is a cascade into and out of the market creating massive bull and bear share price movements. This has been happening since the dawn of time in one way or another. Here is an excellent example of a documented **Dutch tulip bulb** craze centuries ago where the public piled into – and later, out of – a hobby flower market.

---

[55] The Chairman of Berkshire Hathaway, and one of the greatest stock market investors of all time. An investor who chose to invest $10,000 in Berkshire Hathaway when Buffett took over in 1965 would have more than $20 million today. His forte is in identifying undervalued companies, and he is well-known for taking very long-term positions in companies he identifies as being good from under- priced investment prospects. Mr. Buffett provides strong evidence that it is possible to consistently outperform the market in the long-term.

The Dutch Tulip Mania

In Holland a "**tulip mania**" occurred that has been extensively studied by psychologists, economists and stock market observers. This unbelievable true story happened many centuries ago—and still happens every day in our stock markets in one market or another around the globe. Just like tulip bulbs centuries ago, single stocks routinely go from record low to record high prices in the markets on all our exchanges around the world.

In 1559, when Swiss naturalist **Conrad Gesner** described the first tulip bulbs in the garden of a Bavarian magistrate, readers fell in love with them. Tulip bulbs soon became a status symbol for the wealthy because they were beautiful and, more importantly, hard to get.

Early bulb buyers were people who truly prized the lovely flowers, but after prices took off, people began to speculate on the possibility of further price increases. These were the same type of people who knew nothing about flowers, just like boxer Braddock who was attracted to the massive 1920s bull market who knew nothing about stocks except that he thought he was going to make some quick money.

The inexperienced tulip bulb "investors" created a high volume of buying and selling activity, and eventually, tulip bulbs were traded across the local stock exchanges. By 1634, the rage over owning tulip bulbs had spread to the middle classes of Dutch society. Merchant shopkeepers began to compete with one another for single tulip bulbs.

How crazy did it get? At the height of tulip mania in 1635, a single tulip bulb sold for a basket of all the following vital consumer goods worth nearly $35,000 today: 4 tons of wheat, 8 tons of rye, 1 bed, 4 oxen, 8 pigs, 12 sheep, 1 suit of clothes,

2 casks of wine, 4 tons of beer, 2 tons of butter, 1,000 pounds of cheese, and 1 silver drinking cup.

Can you imagine spending $35,000 for a single tulip bulb? I sure can't. But I couldn't imagine spending the kind of money people were on startup internet stocks at the end of the 1990's, either! This was happening routinely in Holland in the mid-17th century. It grew so out of hand that people were selling everything they owned—their homes, their livestock, everything—for the privilege of owning tulips, on the expectation that the bulbs they bought today would be worth a lot more tomorrow. As a result, tulip prices (in today's dollars) ranged from $17,000 all the way up to $76,000 per bulb.

By 1636, tulip bulbs were traded on the Amsterdam stock exchange (along with shares of stock in the Dutch East Indies Company) as well as other equity exchanges in Holland and Europe. Popular interest in tulip bulbs had shifted from hobbyists and collectors to inexperienced public investors and gamblers. People from all walks of life liquidated their homes and other real estate at low prices to speculate in tulip trading—just as people jumped into the end of the equity bull market at the end of the 1990's.

Tulip notaries and clerks were appointed to record transactions. Public laws and regulations were developed to control the craze. In 1636, inexperienced public investors began to liquidate their tulip holdings. Tulip prices weakened, slowly at first, and then rapidly. Public confidence was soon destroyed, and panic seized the market. Within six weeks, tulip prices crashed by 90%—the market bubble burst. Defaults on contracts and liens on tulip bulb speculators were widespread. The market crash left many families bankrupt—the heavy yet consistent price of financial inexperience throughout written history.

Dr. Mark Schwartz, Dr. Bill Garner and host relax after a vibrant panel discussion on pharmaceutical and biopharma startups in Puerto Rico.

The Ponzi Scheme

Nobel laureate economist **Bob Shiller** of Yale University explains the bizarre behavior of inexperienced public investors through the Ponzi scheme for illustration. The Ponzi scheme was a con job perpetrated on the public in 1920 that induced the same frenzy behavior in rising bull markets and the desperate rush to sell in bear markets.

Carlo "Charles" Ponzi was born in Parma, Italy, in 1882. He immigrated to the United States in November of 1903. Over the next 14 years, Ponzi wandered from city to city and from job to job. He worked as a dishwasher, waiter, store clerk and as an Italian interpreter. In 1917, he settled in Boston, where he took a job typing and answering foreign mail. Ponzi invented a mechanism in 1919 to make himself vastly wealthy at the expense of his investors. His approach to stealing money made his name synonymous with **high-yield investment** con jobs.

At the time, Ponzi was considering publishing an export magazine. He had written a letter about the proposed publication to a gentleman in Spain. When Ponzi received the reply, the man had included an **international postal reply coupon.** The idea behind this enclosure was very simple. All Ponzi had to do was take the coupon to his local post office and exchange it for American postage stamps. He could then use the American stamps to send the magazine to Spain.

Tip: Buy stock low in share price in good companies when the public is afraid of the market. Buffett frequently repeats to the press the deep wisdom of British Baron Nathan Rothschild with *"the time to buy is when there's blood in the streets."*

Ponzi noticed that the postal coupon had been purchased in Spain for about one cent in American funds. Yet, when he cashed it in, he was able to get six American one-cent stamps. Thoughts of riches whirled about his mind. He could buy $100 worth of stamps in Spain and then cash them in for $600 worth of stamps in the United States. He also knew that he could not get this kind of interest at a bank.

Ponzi's mind quickly went into overdrive as he devised a clever scheme to capitalize on his idea. He was determined to become a rich man no matter the cost. His first step was to convert his American dollars into Italian (or any other currency where the exchange rate was profitable). Charles Ponzi then claimed that he had found foreign agents who were using the money to purchase international postal coupons in countries with weak currencies. The stamp coupons were supposedly exchanged back into a strong foreign currency and finally back into American funds. He claimed that his net profit on all these transactions was in excess of 400%. It sounded reasonable.

He couldn't do what he was claiming. The red tape of dealing with a bunch of different country postal organizations and the long delays in transferring currency would have destroyed all of Ponzi's promised profits. Mr. Ponzi began bragging to everyone he knew about his high-yield investment program. Nonetheless, friends and family members easily understood what he was saying and they wanted in.

On December 26, 1919, Ponzi filed an application with the Boston city clerk establishing his new business as **The Security Exchange Company** before the SEC existed. He promised 50% interest in 90 days, and the world wanted in. Word spread very quickly about Ponzi's idea and, within a few months, the lines outside the door of his office grew long. Thousands of people purchased Ponzi's promissory notes, paying $10 to $50,000 each. The average investment people made with Ponzi was $300 (which equates to over $3,000 today).

Why would so many people pay into a scheme that didn't work? The reason was that the early investors obtained great returns on their money. Ponzi used the money from later investors to pay off his earlier obligations. It was a new twist on the age-old pyramid scheme.

With an estimated income of $1,000,000 per week—$10 million a week in today's money—at the height of his scheme, his newly-hired staff couldn't take the money in fast enough. They were filling desk drawers, wastepaper baskets and closets in the office with investors' cash. He opened branches.

Copycat schemes popped up quickly across New England as other fraudsters caught wind of Ponzi's success.

By the early summer of 1920, Ponzi had taken in millions and began to live the life of a very rich man. Ponzi dressed in the finest of suits, had dozens of gold-handled canes, showered his wife in jewels and purchased a 20-room mansion.

From the start, regulators were suspicious; federal, state, and local authorities investigated him. Yet no one could pin Ponzi with a single charge of wrongdoing. Ponzi had managed to pay off all of his notes in the 45 days he had promised. Since everyone was happy to get their profits, not a single complaint had been filed.

On July 26, 1920, Ponzi's house of cards began to collapse. The *Boston Post* headlined a story on the front page questioning the legitimacy of Ponzi's scheme. Later that day, the District suspended him from taking in new investments until an auditor had examined his books.

Within hours, crowds of people lined up outside Ponzi's door demanding return of investment. Ponzi obliged, assuring the public that his organization was financially stable and that he could meet all obligations. He returned the money to those that requested it. By the end of the first day, he had settled nearly 1,000 claims with the panicked crowd.

By continuing to meet his obligations, the angry masses began to dwindle and public support swelled. Crowds followed Ponzi's every move. He was urged by many to enter politics and was hailed as a hero. Loud cheers and applause assured him of public confidence. People were eager just to touch his hand.

Ponzi continued to dream and scheme. He had planned to establish a new type of bank where the profits would be split equally between the shareholders and the depositors. He also planned to reopen his company under a new name, the **Charles Ponzi Company**, whose main purpose was to invest in major industries around the world.

The public continued to support him until August 10, 1920. On that day, the auditors, banks, and newspapers declared Ponzi bankrupt. Two days later, Ponzi confessed that he had a criminal record, which worsened his situation. In 1908, he had served 20 months in a Canadian prison on forgery charges related to a similar high-yield investment scheme. This was followed in 1910 by an additional two-year sentence in Atlanta for smuggling five Italians over the Canadian border into the United States.

On August 13, Ponzi was arrested by federal authorities and released on $25,000 bond. Just moments later, he was re-arrested by Massachusetts authorities and re-released on an additional $25,000 bond.

The Ponzi scheme turned into a mess for the public. There were federal legal suits, state civil suits, criminal trials, bankruptcy hearings, individual law suits against Ponzi and countersuits filed back by Ponzi. Five different banks collapsed in the aftermath. At least 40,000 people had paid $15 million (about $151 million in inflation-adjusted U.S. money today) into Ponzi's scheme. A final audit of his books concluded that he had taken in enough money to buy approximately 180 million postal coupons, yet auditors could only confirm the purchase of just two.

Ponzi's only legitimate source of income over the period was $45 he received as a dividend of five shares of telephone stock. His remaining assets totaled to $1,593,834.12, which was a tenth of the outstanding debt. It took about eight years, but those sucked in recovered a meager 37% of their investment in installments gradually just in time to lose it again in the 1929 stock market crash!

UBS Attorney Carlos Pou, CEO Dave Watkins of FeedYak.com, and Attorney Daniel Hall of RealFastResults.com relax in the afternoon of the Puerto Rico Investment Summit of 2016.

Irrational Exuberance

Nobel Laureate Robert Shiller explains in his book *Irrational Exuberance* that it is completely rational for inexperienced public investors to behave in the stock market like tulip bulb or postal reply coupon investors. He explains that such people are attracted into a rising stock market or single stock if they have heard of windfall profits of family, friends, acquaintances or even media accounts of the sort. The inexperienced public investor rationalizes that if another likeminded person has made money in a specific stock, if they buy at today's prices, shares will probably be worth more tomorrow.

Shiller explains that this is rational in the middle of an extended bull move in a single stock, but is very dangerous at the top when smart money has sold out. When the bull market collapses like a house of cards, the public sells in panic and dramatic crashes occur—the 1929 to 1933, 2000 to 2003, 2007 to 2008 drops are examples.

Maggie Mahar, a Yale English professor and first-rate financial journalist, describes what happens to the trustingly unwary at the top of a market in her book *Bull!*:

> *While insiders bailed out, most small investors did not sell. They did what they were told [by Wall Street], "buy and hold," doubling their bets all the way up. The higher the most aggressive growth [mutual] funds rose, the greater their allure. In 1999 investors wagered twice as much on these funds as they had in 1996 and 1997 put together. Even after the NASDAQ began its long slide, investors continued to chase the last best thing— at the end of 2000 individuals were investing in aggressive growth funds at more than twice the rate as they had in 1999.*

> *As always, when a bull market ends, those who could afford it least lost the most. In Massachusetts, Sharon Cassidy, a divorced college professor who had single-handedly put her four children through college, began to step up saving for her own retirement in 1990. By then she was 52, and earning roughly $42,000 a year. Listening to the financial advisors who visited her college, she stashed most of her money in broad-based*

equity funds, and, by the end of 1998, she had managed to accumulate over $350,000. At that point, she felt she was in sight of her goal: retirement in four years, at age 62, with $500,000.

When the market skidded, she held on. "I felt I had no other choice," said Cassidy. Then the bear showed his claws. By the end of 2001, at age 63, she was forced to rethink her life plan. "If I work until I'm 70, I can retire with $400,000" she said. I'm lucky – I like my work, and $400,000 is a lot more than most people have. But I'm angry, angry at myself and angry at the people who advised me."

EXPERIENCED INVESTORS

Experienced investors are a different breed altogether from the inexperienced. An individual who has ridden through an extended bull market and perhaps lost—or at least witnessed the financial carnage wreaked upon the public investor—has an altogether different perspective on the market.

These are the big winners in the public, those wise enough from experience to buy stocks low and hold for long periods of time and then sell when the signs are obvious insiders are selling out with windfall profits.

Here is a description of this by **Maggie Mahar** from her book *Bull!*:

As the market heated up, experienced investors knew, with a sinking certainty, that the big caps were rising too high, too fast. In the three years ending in December 1998, Dell alone shot up 3,197%. With the benefit of hindsight, market watchers would point out that the broad market peaked in 1998 and that the first phase of the bear market began in August or September of 1999. By the fall of 1999, insiders were bailing out en masse. Once again, **Richard Russell,** *editor of* **Richard Russell's Dow Theory Letter,** *sounded a warning.* "Holding for the long-term works beautifully in a bull market. In a major bear market, it is absolutely disastrous policy," *Russell told his subscribers in October of 1999.*

CORPORATE EXECUTIVE INSIDERS

The insider that you will hear about in the popular financial press is the corporate executive. This first class of **insider** successfully gains control of the **board of directors** of a publicly traded corporation. They do this to obtain large gifts of **employee stock options,** pay and benefit packages.

The corporate executive insider does everything possible to get the price of the stock to go up over the next few years as their options vest. They use news leaked to the media and also use legally (or illegally) **misleading financial statements** to draw in **inexperienced public investors**.

Tip: Buy low when nobody you know is looking at the stock market. Sell high when everybody you know wants into the stock market!

For example, **America Online (AOL)** corporate executive insider Bob Pittman used both Wall Street and the general media effectively to promote AOL as the bull market heated up in 1996: *"During Pittman's first full year as president AOL held twice as many analyst conference calls and received 10 to 20 times the coverage in media and* *entertainment publications as any other company in its then-peer set, which included Yahoo and Lycos."*[56]

In addition, the inside corporate executives at AOL were "cooking the accounting books" to intentionally mislead investors into believing that the company was profitable. This was done to seduce inexperienced investors into buying more stock to pump up the share price so that insiders could dump their holdings of stock on the public. These executives had acquired their stock at low, low prices with their free employee stock options gifted from a corporate board of directors they controlled.

Lisa Buyer, a fund manager at T. Rowe Price, said about AOL in the fall of '95: *"What the shorts [short sellers] can't understand is that Wall Street, witnessing such growth, is willing to overlook the company's losses and well-known aggressive accounting methods."*[57] The "growth", however, that she was talking about was a growth in the number of subscribers, not a growth in earnings. The cost of acquiring those customers was so high that AOL had not, in fact, yet earned a profit—though, thanks to its creative accounting, it was reporting profits. Nobody in the public knew that AOL insiders were hiring themselves out to teach other executives how to cook their books—they were proud of their skill at deceiving the public.

The employee stock option was intended to retain highly skilled employees critical to key engineering and production

---

[56] Amy P. Hutton, "Four Rules for Taking Your Message to Wall Street," *Harvard Business Review*, May 2001, 125.

[57] Linda Sandler and Jared Sandberg, "Heard on the Street: America Online Lures Investors, Dismays Shorts," *The Asian Wall Street Journal*, 13 November 1995, 15.

processes of the firm. The idea has been poorly implemented. Options flow straight to the top of the corporate pyramid. Today, employee stock options are the biggest corporate governance problem in the field of finance. In 2000, the Bureau of Labor looked at who received options in 1999 and found that, nationwide, Just 1.7% of non-executive private sector employees received any stock options and only 4.6% of executives received them—93.7% went up to the CEO.

CEO Richard Carrion of Banco Popular de Puerto Rico (NYSE: BPOP) is a strong supporter of the UPR-RP School of Business, the only AACSB accredited program in the Caribbean. Just 5% of Business Schools worldwide are AACSB Accredited.

In 1999—a banner year for employee stock option exercise—98% of all U.S. workers of publicly traded corporations did not receive a single stock option as part of their pay. At the end of '99, the CEOs running the 800 largest companies in the United States were sitting on "fully vested" options worth $18 billion. They could cash them in at any time when they knew they had driven the market up as high as they could—and this is exactly what they did.

Even more sinister, a 1999 study by the Federal Reserve of 138 firms estimated that, by legally not accounting for the value of corporate executive employee stock options, the companies had falsely boosted their profits by 10.5%—the managers walked away with a big cut of the owner's profits. Do you trust P/E ratios now? I hope not. This has occurred because inside corporate executives have been successful in garnering the support of Washington, through executive special interest groups, to stop the SEC's attempt to force corporations to show executive options as a cost to the company.

INSTITUTIONAL INVESTORS

These managers buy stock low to dump later on an eager, overly-optimistic, inexperienced public. I first learned of these investors when I began studying the history of the stock market. These individuals still operate to this day in teams to buy up (corner) the supply (float) of a company's stock. They created investment pools notorious as part of the corruption on Wall Street. These investment pools were renamed mutual funds after the depression to get the public to forget a very murky past. Hedge funds pool the money of the 1%.

Market Corners

Market corners are defined as *"a market condition brought about intentionally – though sometimes accidentally – when virtually all the purchasable, or floating, supply of a company's stock is held by an individual or group who are thus able to dictate the price when settlement is called.*"[58] A market corner is an extreme form of **short squeeze**, where the buy side of the market has almost complete control of all floating (purchasable) shares. A 2006 academic finance article from Wharton finds strong evidence that large investors and corporate insiders possessed enough market power before 1933 to manipulate stock prices through a market corner.[59] They make it clear in their article that *"one of the main hurdles in studying market manipulation is that the data are hard to obtain since the activity is often illegal and thus participants do their best to hide it."* The article by professor Franklin Allen of Wharton further notes that *"although stock markets are far better regulated today than in the 19th century, market manipulations by large investors and insiders still occur around the world."*

A Brief History of the Market Corner

The favorite tool of the robber baron, was the **bear corner.**

These financially powerful men were in a special position to hoodwink unwary investors because they were corporate officers as well as large stockholders. These manipulators often controlled a huge amount of the common shares of stock—often more than the float at the time they forced settlement—allowing them to dictate the share price the short sellers had to pay. Stock prices gapped when the stock was cornered causing huge increases with no intermediate price points around the corner date. The amount of wealth

---

[58] Wyckoff, P., 1972, *Wall Street and the Stock Market: A Chronology* (1644-1971), Philadelphia: Chilton Book Company.

[59] F. Allen, L. Litov and J. Mei,*"Large Investors, Price Manipulation, and Limits to Arbitrage: An Anatomy of Market Corners"*, Working Paper 06-02, Wharton Financial Institutions Center, University of Pennsylvania.

controlled by the manipulators was also large compared to the market capitalization of the stock.[60]

It was easier for these men to corner the market back then. It was also a lot easier to take a short position. According to John Gordon, *"Most short sellers were not affected by borrowing the stock as is done today. But by using seller's options stock was often sold for future delivery within a specified time, usually 10, 20, or 30 days, with the precise time of delivery up to either the seller — or buyer in which case it was called a buyer's option. These "options" differed from modern options — puts and calls — in that the puts and calls convey only a right, not an obligation to complete the contract."*

The manipulator bought large quantities of seller's options from short sellers through various agents. After buying all the seller's options in the float, the robber baron could force a corner by exercising his right for immediate delivery. The manipulator then waited for the delivery from bearish investors who had sold the "seller's option" under legal obligation to tender shares. Cornelius Vanderbilt purchased all floating shares as well as all "sellers' options" during the Hudson River Corner.[61]

---

[60] Cornelius Vanderbilt, for instance, put together a stock pool of $5 million in cash for the second Harlem corner. At the time, he already owned a large block of Harlem stocks from the first Harlem corner. On March 29, 1864, Harlem had a market capitalization of $11.9 million with 110,000 shares outstanding. By the end of April, Vanderbilt and his allies in the pool owned 137,000 shares, with the difference sold to them by short sellers. At the time of his death, Vanderbilt left an estate to his heirs worth $90 million. See Gordon, J. 1999, *The Great Game: The Emergence of Wall Street as a World Power: 1653-2000*, New York: Touchstone.

[61] In the second Harlem corner, Vanderbilt was so furious at the short sellers, led by Daniel Drew, that he was planning to drive the stock price up to $1,000 per share. He dropped the plan after he found out that this would bankrupt almost all brokerage firms on Wall Street. See Clews, H. 1888, *Twenty Years in Wall Street*, New York: Irving Publishing Co.

Margin requirements were also less restrictive. The most Wall Street will lend investors today is 50% margin. Prior to 1934 when Roosevelt enacted the Securities Act, margin was nego-tiated between brokers and cli-ents. It could be as low as 10%, This allowed the manipulator to acquire large blocks of stocks with relatively little capital. Corporations faced no financial reporting requirements to stock-holders whatsoever. The general public had very little knowledge

Fact: The stock market crash did indeed spark the Great Depression, but the causes are thought by economists to be much broader. They include distressed key industries, an end to the real estate boom, and widespread bad loans leading to massive banking failures.

about the float of a particular stock—or even who the major stockholders were – let alone how much stock they owned.

Because of this, short sellers had a false sense of security when they shorted a stock, not realizing that the float was often far smaller than they had thought—meaning the stock price would shoot up, not down. There were other reasons for the restricted float. Poor transportation made it difficult for out of town and overseas investors to bring their shares to market— effectively taking their equity securities out of the float. In 1869, for instance, foreigners owned $243 million in railroad stock shares, but were not a concern to manipulators during this period when many railroad stocks were cornered.[62]

The legal system was much more corrupt than it is today and judges could be bribed by manipulators to issue injunctions to restrict the issue of new shares. By controlling the supply of new shares, it made it a lot easier for the manipulator to

---

62   Sobel, R., 1988, *Panic on Wall Street*, Truman Talley Books.

achieve a corner. In addition, there was a blatant disregard for director conflicts of interests and minority shareholder rights. Directors often took advantage of their position to manipulate the stock price because they were able to restrict the supply of shares. All of these reasons made corners easier in the 19th century. Despite this, people get caught doing them today.

Hudson River Corner (1863)

The **Hudson River Railroad** was built despite strong opposition from both the Harlem Railroad and the Vanderbilt

Annie Mustafa, MBA (Assistant to Secretary Bacó) discusses the program with Dr. Brown as Attorneys Daniel Hall and Michael Juarbe Laffitte (of the Puerto Rico Department of Commerce and Economic Development) chat in the background.

steamboat interests. It was constructed on the east bank of the Hudson River and reached to east Albany by 1851. The main passenger depot was located at Tenth Avenue and 30th Street on the West Side of Manhattan.

By the summer of 1863, Cornelius Vanderbilt owned a substantial block of stock in the Hudson but was still primarily interested in the Harlem. This changed when a group of traders began selling the Hudson short. Vanderbilt then participated in a scheme (which he suggested) to convince the "shorts" that the supporters of the Hudson were lacking in cash. "Supporters" sold large blocks of stock to the "shorts" for cash with an option to buy back the shares within 30 days at a slightly higher price. Instead of holding the stock, the "shorts" immediately sold it.

The "supporters" then quietly bought the stock the "shorts" sold along with all other shares in the market. By July 1863, the stock of the Hudson was cornered and the shorts took a bath. Vanderbilt and his allies took control of the board of directors of the Hudson in 1864. Cornelius Vanderbilt became president of the railroad in 1865.

The First Harlem Corner (1863)[63]

At the beginning of 1863, **Cornelius Vanderbilt** purchased enough stock in the **Harlem City Railway**—from $8 to $9 per share—to have a controlling interest. Cornelius was well known as an iron-fisted but outstanding business manager in both the ocean and rail transportation industries—if you were a stock investor in railways, you would have been very happy to have him managing the firm. He began actively managing the company, and its stock rose to $50 per share. In April 1863, the New York City Council passed an ordinance allowing the Harlem City Railway to build a streetcar system along the length of Broadway. Investors reasoned that the large increase of paying passengers would boost the company's profits. The stock price soon soared to $75 per share.

---

[63] Allen, F., and D. Gale, 1992, "Stock Price Manipulation," *Review of Financial Studies*, Vol. 5:503-529.

Daniel Drew was a manipulator who preferred to force stock prices down—bull corners—by short-selling a stock. Drew was a member of the highly corrupt New York City Council for this very reason. He and all other council members sold the stock short and then, as council members, voted to repeal the Broadway railroad extension ordinance to force the share price down.

Vanderbilt got wind of the manipulation scheme and used secret agents to quietly buy up the remaining floating stock. The share price shot up again since Vanderbilt now owned all the stock. When the members of the New York City Council tried to cover their short positions buying shares back, they found out that there was none available for sale. Cornelius forced them to settle for $179 per share, a loss of $104 per share for the short sellers. Daniel Drew himself lost over a half a million dollars in Vanderbilt's bear squeeze revenge. Without dealing with short sellers like Daniel Drew, Cornelius had set himself up for a profit of $66 per share, or 733%. His profit was actually much higher when he won out control of the corporation.

The Second Harlem Corner (1864)[64]

By 1864, the Harlem City Railway stock price had settled down to about $150 per share because the Broadway extension still had not been approved. Vanderbilt was furious with the corruption of the **New York City Council**. He decided to go directly to the New York State Legislature in Albany to get the extension down Broadway approved for the Harlem City Railway in the form of a state bill. Daniel Drew was mad, too, and wanted revenge against Cornelius.

Drew talked state legislators into doing a bull squeeze with him by spreading rumors the bill was going to pass. The good news drove up the Harlem City Railway stock, and Daniel Drew began selling it short. He had also talked the state legislators

---

[64] Clews, H., 1888, *Twenty Years in Wall Street*, New York: Irving Publishing Co.

into secretly planning to defeat the bill even though they were spreading lies that they were going to pass it. The defeat of the bill forced the stock price down from $150 to $100 in two days.

Vanderbilt was furious (he was known for his bad temper and mean nature) and overbought shares of the Harlem City Railway. This shut off the supply of the stock and, as per the law of supply and demand, the share price skyrocketed. Cornelius forced the short sellers to settle at $285. Daniel Drew lost over a half million dollars again.

The Prairie du Chien Corner (1865)[65]

At the same time that Daniel Drew—the bear—and Cornelius Vanderbilt—the bull—were fighting it out in New York, the birth of the mutual fund had come in the form of the investment pool. An enterprising bullish investment pool operator, **William Marston**, was becoming very wealthy organizing stock market corners with a small group of investors. By November 6, 1865, he had gained control of the entire 29,880 share-outstanding float of **Prairie du Chien Railroad Company** and just as much short interest.

Mr. Marston, as leader of the bull pool, called for settlement that very morning and drove the stock price straight up. *The New York Times* reported this to be *"one of the sharpest, and beyond all precedent, the most sudden corners known to the 40-year history of the New York Stock Exchange."*

The Michigan Southern Corner (1866)[66]

Daniel Drew was caught in another bear squeeze when the **Michigan Southern Railroad** was cornered by inside

---

[65] See *New York Times*, 11/07/1865, Financial Affairs section.

[66] Chancellor, E., 2000, *Devil Take the Hindmost: A History of Financial Speculation*, New York: Plume Books., Chapter 6.

Trap: Shakeouts are forceful temporary breaks in an uptrend. They are gut wrenching and require courage to ride through or buy into.

executive directors of the railroad. Per *The New York Times* of April 6, 1866, *"the Street was enlivened today (referring to April 5) by one of those extraordinary special movements in the railway market which will periodically occur on the bull side of the speculation, as it more frequently occurs on the bear side of the speculation…the cash stock was at no time made scarce for delivery up to yesterday afternoon (April 4). The case appeared to be different this morning, judging from the eagerness and excitement at the early Board."* This source also points out that one of the manipulators had reportedly been a director of Michigan Southern Railroad: *"two of the three prominent managers (in the cornering clique) are said to have been notorious bankrupts, whose paper is in every man's pocketbook, and the third a prominent official of the road, whose speculations have been so flagrant that a bill has been introduced into the legislature to check them."*

Apparently the cornering pool was well organized, because Daniel Drew filed with the Supreme Court seeking an injunction against the firm of Scott, Capron, & Co. (lenders of the Michigan Southern stock to Daniel Drew). *The New York Times* noted that *"the plaintiff (Drew) is informed and believes that the defendants (Scott, Capron & Co.) are a party to the said fraud and conspiracy, and desire and intend thereby to defraud and injure the plaintiff."*

The Failed Erie Corner (March 1868)

Erie Railroad was under the control of Daniel Drew and Jay Gould. Cornelius Vanderbilt decided that he wanted it. Cornelius was very confident he could acquire control because he had beaten the tar out of Drew and Gould in the Harlem City Railroad stock market battles. He now had allies in a group of Boston capitalists who owned a large block of Erie Railroad shares of stock. Vanderbilt poured millions into the purchase of the stock. He believed he had completely cornered the equity issue. He had bought more shares than were in existence.

Brian Tennenbaum, J.D. and Doc Brown discuss local real estate development opportunities. Attorney Daniel Hall J.D. of RealFastResults.com and Annie Mustafa, MBA of the Puerto Rico Department of Commerce and Economic development listen in.

Daniel Drew was ready this time after dealing with Cornelius Vanderbilt in the Harlem City Railroad corner. As a director of the board of the company, he surprised Vanderbilt by converting a large issue of convertible bonds into common stocks and flooded the market with these new shares. Vanderbilt's corner was broken by the sudden increase in float that dropped the price. He lost $7 million. Cornelius Vanderbilt was infuriated with Daniel Drew, and scheming to get even.

The Erie Corner (November 1868)[67]

Daniel Drew and Jay Gould worked out a scheme to short the Erie Railroad and other stocks in a **bear raid**, another term for a bull squeeze. They then tried to force the margin rates to rise to cause a general stock market decline by withdrawing lots of money from New York banks. Jay was more aggressive and ruthless than Daniel, who was skeptical that they could have a significant impact on interest rates and, even so, if that would affect the stock market significantly in the short term.

Daniel Drew began to waver in withdrawing his money from the banks. Jay Gould, angry at Daniel Drew for backing out switched his strategy from a bear raid to a bull run; switching from short selling to buying up stock. Drew had no idea that he had been betrayed and kept on selling short the Erie Railroad stock, completely unaware that it was actually his "trusted partner" who was buying it all up.

The share price for Erie Railroad stock dropped from $50 to $40 in October and fell further to $35 on November 13. But by then Gould had secretly bought up the entire float of stock. On November 16, the price suddenly jumped to $55 and caught Drew short 70,000 shares.

The Failed Gold Corner (1869)

The value of money used to be guaranteed through the gold standard. The advantages of the commodity backed

---

[67] Sharp, R., 1989, *The Lore and Legends of Wall Street*, Homewood, IL.: Dow Jones-Irwin.

currency were that it imposed a common standard of value for all money and imposed economic discipline on countries. This meant that countries would horde gold and only a limited amount could float for industrial purposes—jewelry, gold plating, dentistry. The gold standard caused just as many problems as it solved. Nations could not protect their industries from foreign competition through import or export restrictions, the growth of a nation's money supply was restricted by its gold stock, and governments were limited in their ability to respond to economic crisis such as rapid unemployment.

This was the time that the problem of trading goods and services with other countries issuing different currencies was solved by using gold as an international standard of value. During the 17th and 18th centuries, major trading nations in Western Europe made their currencies freely convertible into gold. Gold bullion could be exported and imported from one country to another without significant restriction. Each unit of currency was defined in terms of grains of fine gold. Nations adopting the **gold standard** agreed to exchange paper money or coins for gold bullion in unlimited amounts at predetermined prices. Gold was too heavy to transport, so this system had its own problems.

The **gold exchange standard** adopted in the 1800's allowed a country's money to be directly converted into foreign currencies. The economic chaos of the worldwide Great Depression in the 1930's caused the gold exchange standard to collapse and the **modified exchange standard** known as the **Bretton Woods System** was developed under the control of an international lender of last resort. The **International Monetary Fund (IMF)** linked all world currencies to gold and the U.S. Dollar. Foreign governments and investors began to lose confidence in the ability of U.S. policymakers to control the

U.S. economy and inflation in the 1960's. This resulted in the collapse of the Bretton Woods System.

In 1971, President Richard Nixon dismantled the failing Bretton Woods System. The 1st world adopted the **floating currency standard** as a universal mechanism of exchange of goods and services. Today, all world monies are **fiat currencies**, a country's coins and paper are not backed by a commodity like gold.

In 1868, the federal government held around $75 million in gold reserves. The floating gold supply was about $20 million. Jay Gould knew that if he could buy up the float, the gold price would soar. Gould conspired with **Abel Corbin**, the brother-in-law of **President Grant**, to influence the government's policy on gold. Abel lobbied Grant to shift policy—a sensitive subject, because gold also anchored the U.S. dollar's value at the time.

It looked like Grant was going to go for it. Gould bought $50 million in gold, driving the price up from $130 to $137 per ounce. Gould then set out on an aggressive lobbying campaign of government officials, but they began to suspect he was trying to corner the market. Gould got a bad feeling that the federal government was on to him and might try to break his corner.

Gould was never invited to high society parties despite his great wealth because of his ruthlessness. He secretly began selling gold while he convinced his friends to buy at any price. By October 4, 1869, feverish purchases of Gould's friends had pushed the price of gold from $140 to $160 per ounce. This was recorded as a **Black Friday**, because hundreds of firms on Wall Street were driven into bankruptcy by the huge price swing. A commodity is widely consumed

Real estate developer and attorney Brian Tennenbaum is the regional director of the Morgan Reed Group in Puerto Rico.

by the public and monitored closely by governments. This makes the manipulation of a commodity market much harder to pull off. For instance, there are less than 50 major futures commodity markets, but there are more than 16,000 stocks trading in North America. It is a lot easier for manipulators to pump up the price of a stock and dump it on the public, because there are fewer people paying attention to a specific stock as compared to a commodity market.

The Failed Erie Corner (1872)

In the summer of 1872, Jay Gould invited Daniel Drew and Henry Smith to join him for a bear raid on Erie Railroad stocks. They schemed to push down the stock price by suddenly withdrawing large deposits from New York banks. This restricted the deposits banks could lend to stock investors on margin. The liquidity crisis restricting margin would make it hard for speculators to buy stock. This reduced the number of buy orders entering the market and reduced upward pressure on prices. This was possible at the time due to the lack of lenders of last resort (now we have the Federal Reserve System). The SEC maintains strict position requirements to spot market manipulation such as this today. Programs run 24 hours a day to spot manipulators around the world. You can research the actual positions of institutional investors online via the form 13F: https://www.sec.gov/fast-answers/answers-form13fhtm.html

Drew turned bullish after the team's initial success to extract revenge on Gould for betrayal in the first Erie Corner. Daniel built a large long position without notifying Gould or Smith. On September 17, he cornered the market by calling for a settlement of all short interests. Gould could deliver the shares of stocks he had borrowed to sell short. The corner impacted the prices of all stocks, which caused a general decline. Gould was mad and came away intent on teaching Daniel Drew a final lesson.

The Northwestern Corner (1872)[68]

Jay Gould tricked Daniel Drew and Henry Smith into joining him for another bear raid by selling Northwestern stock short. They didn't suspect that Gould was going to try to trick them. They kept selling the Northwestern Railway stock short while Gould built up a long position buying as much as he could. Smith grew suspicious as the share price rose unabated. He acquired a warrant from a judge for Gould's arrest on charges of looting the Erie Railroad treasury that Gould controlled.

---

[68] See *New York Times*, November 26th, 1872 and also Chancellor (2000), page 171.

Gould wriggled out of the charges and decided to ruin Drew and Smith by cornering the market for Northwestern even more. The price soared from $80 to $230 in a few days, then Gould forced them to settle their short positions at that price. The corner had a serious impact on all stocks, as people sold their holdings to buy into the rapid price increases of the Northwestern Railway stock. Astute investors who noticed that this was a rising stock and had the courage to buy it cheap walked away with a huge profit.

The Northern Pacific Corner (1901)[69]

In the spring of 1901, J.P. Morgan fought with a group of investors led by **Edward Harriman** for the control of the **Northern Pacific Railroad**—which would lead to the control of all railroad freight receipts and fares to the Pacific coast. Harriman started by acquiring $40 million in common stock, running just short of 40,000 shares of gaining control. J.P. Morgan got wind of the scheme and, in a panic, rushed to acquire the remaining float of stock. His large purchases sent prices soaring from $114 to $147 per share in five days.

A group of short sellers noticed the unusual increase in price and built a large short interest in the stock. On May 9, short sellers realized that they were caught in a bear squeeze from both Harriman's corner and Morgan's response. The price went from $170 to a record level of $1,000 during the day. The market for other stocks plummeted, since short sellers were hard pressed to cover their positions by selling their other assets.[70] The trading volume was 3,336,000 shares for the

---

[69] Thomas, D., 1989, *The Plungers and the Peacocks: an Update of the Classic History of the Stock Market*, New York: William Morrow and Company, Inc.
[70] Kyle, A., and W. Xiong, 2001, "Contagion as a Wealth Effect," *Journal of Finance*, Vol. 56: 1401-1440 develop a model that captures this contagion effect.

day, a record not broken until 1925. Morgan and Harriman agreed to settle with the short sellers at $150 the next day. It was very dangerous to short sell, even back when it was easier to do it. Today it is harder to short shares. Buy puts to accomplish the same goal.

The Stutz Motor Company of America, Inc. Corner (1920)[71]

Tip: One of the great advantages of ETFs is that you can buy ETF put stock options to hedge against any unexpected general breaks in the stock market that might cause a loss in your stock portfolio.

Allan Ryan was a well-known short squeeze market manipulator in the early 20th century. He bought a controlling interest in the Stutz Motor Company and acquired a position on the board of directors. Mr. Stutz, the founder, hated him for his dishonest business practices and sold out—a bitter departure for an automobile legend whose cars are still prized by collectors today. Ryan began marketing Stutz cars with overly-optimistic promises beyond what the company could actually deliver.

Ryan continued to buy the float, and the company's stock price rose from $100 to $134 per share. Ryan was informed that short sellers, who included some prominent members of the New York Stock Exchange, had taken action because the price had risen too high. To counter the bears, Ryan borrowed a substantial amount of money to buy additional

---

[71] Brooks, J., 1969, *Once in a Golconda: A True Drama of Wall Street 1920-1938*, New York: Harper and Row.

shares of the company stock. At first, despite Ryan's large purchase, the stock price went down—since the short-selling pressure was high—but the price finally responded upward in March, reaching $391.

Toward the end of March, short sellers were selling stock that had to be borrowed from Ryan because he had accumulated nearly all of the floating shares. On March 31, the Governing committee of the NYSE announced it had decided to suspend all dealings in Stutz Motor stock for an indefinite period due to irregular price movements.

On April 20, the Protective Committee of the NYSE announced that it was ready to accept impartial mediation that led to a settlement for the short sellers at the price of $550. Shortly after this fiasco, the NYSE quietly amended its constitution by allowing the governing committee to postpone the time for deliveries on short contracts with the purpose of preventing corners.

Ryan's bad management eventually ran Stutz Motor Company into bankruptcy.

The Piggly-Wiggly Corner (1932)

Piggly-Wiggly is a supermarket chain founded in the Midwest by a grocery clerk who noticed that it would be far more efficient for shoppers to peruse aisles and pay in checkouts instead of dealing with a clerk at a grocery counter. Clarence Saunders was fired for repeatedly suggesting the idea to his boss, but eventually founded the first supermarket chain. In 1923, he wanted to make a seasoned equity offering, but also intended to bring in as much cash as he could for it. Clarence got greedy.

He hired Jesse Livermore, a well-known stock manipulator, to push up the share price in the secondary market before issuing the new stock. Mr. Livermore was very successful in driving up the price, but the trading volume and the fast rise attracted substantial short interest, which eventually led to a bear squeeze in mid-March. Given his large position, **Clarence Saunders** thought that he could make more money by canceling his previous plan to issue more stocks and thus make the bears pay more.

In early 1932, Merrill Lynch and other bear interests on Wall Street hammered the price of Piggly-Wiggly stock. Saunders took a train to New York City with $2 million in cash in a small bag and fought back. Clarence bought Piggly-Wiggly stock until he had orders for 196,000 of the 200,000 outstanding shares. Pressured by the bulls, the stock price soared 50 points on March 23. The next day, the New York Stock Exchange declared a 'corner' existed and de-listed the stock. The NYSE gave the 'bears' five days rather than the normal 24 hours to deliver the stock. Saunders had bought forgetting that bear interest Merrill Lynch was a prominent and influential member of the NYSE.

Saunders' bank and his friends were put under pressure to sell under any terms and the price of Piggly Wiggly tanked. Clarence Saunders was driven into bankruptcy from being forced to sell all his stock in the company he had founded at a loss. On October 15, 1953, Clarence Saunders died in his pink palace http://www.memphis-museums.org/pink-palace-museum/about/the-mansion/. Having built and lost two fortunes, he is the man who brought the retail store into the 20th century. He was a well-known corporate inside executive at the time and was well liked by the public.

The Radio Corporation of America Corner (1928)

William C. Durant was a millionaire in the horse-drawn carriage business before taking over the Buick Motor Company. He then created General Motors and Chevrolet. In 1927, William Durant decided to manipulate the share price of RCA, Radio Corporation of America. He noticed that the bulk of shares RCA had issued were held by RCA itself, General Electric, Westinghouse and several other big corporations. More importantly, these shares were not traded—they were not in float. In addition, there was a lot of hype in the market for RCA since its radio transmission was considered a revolution in communications technology at the time.

Durant started a pool to accumulate RCA stock. Because of the feverish purchases of the Durant cornering group, they soon bought all floating shares and all shares sold short. Their trading generated a daily turnover of more than 500,000 shares, while officially there were only 400,000 shares actually available for purchase in float. The pool forced the market into a technical corner in March 1928. The corner was unintentional, because the Durant group was simply trying to manipulate the price of the stock upwards. They weren't trying to gain control of the firm. They never controlled a large part of the shares and could never call the shorts to settle. The short sellers suffered, though; from March 12, the bears started struggling to settle their accounts and the price skyrocketed more than $61 in just four days. The enormous profit Durant extracted from this corner helped him form General Motors.

Anti-Corner Regulations

Several legal and regulatory developments have made corners more difficult. For instance, the **NYSE and Open Board Rule** of 1868 required corporations to register all securities

Fact: A "stag" is an investor who buys and sells stocks rapidly to make quick profits.

sold at the exchange and provide 30-day notice on any new issues. This made the float of the company public knowledge. This came about because the legislative committee of the NYSE launched an investigation of corners, from an increased concern of members of the "Big Board" on the negative impact on market transactions.

The 1934 Securities Act imposed a mandatory margin requirement of between 50% and 75% under the control of the Federal Reserve Board, which increased the capital needed to control large blocks of stock. Then, in 1968, the **Williams Act** required the filing with the SEC of any one person or group of persons who have acquired a beneficial ownership of more than 5% of equity of a stock issue within 10 days of share acquisition—is now 2 business days.

The **Governing Committee of the New York Stock Exchange** de-listed Stutz Motors after its corner in 1920, setting a stern precedence that effectively voided the contract between short seller and manipulator. Delisting prevents manipulators who are caught from distributing their position at the stock exchange to short-sellers after the corner. Manipulators can still profit from high prices short-sellers have to pay for the borrowed shares but, with this rule, they lost the liquidity to sell their vast holdings they had enjoyed before 1920. As a result, the Stutz Motor corner was the last publicly detected intentional corner on the New York Stock Exchange.

Contemporary Corners

Stock markets are better regulated today than in the 19th century, but market manipulations by large investors still occur in all stock exchanges around the world. Only the blatant cases make it into press. For instance, in August 2004, Citigroup sold more than 200 different Euro-zone bonds in the space of 2 minutes.[72] After the price fell, Citi traders bought it all back again at a lower price netting around 15 million Euros in profit. Citi came to press because trades were heavily scrutinized by market authorities—rapid short selling substantially restricted market liquidity, causing major problems for other investors.

In May 1991, a bond trader at Salomon Brothers was discovered attempting to corner the market in two-year U.S. Treasury notes. During the 1990's bull market, numerous price manipulation schemes for penny stocks—stocks trading under $5 per share—were discovered by the SEC.

In 2002, China's worst stock-market crime was a scheme to manipulate the share price of a firm called China Venture Capital. Seven people, including two of the firm's former executives, were accused of using $700 million and 1,500 brokerage accounts nationwide to manipulate the company share price upward. The copper futures market was manipulated upward by a rogue trader at the Japanese trading firm Sumitomo.

The record of publicly recorded market corners indicates that they were very quick, occurring over a few days or a few months. This attracted undesirable **stags** into the market for

---

[72] Bonds issued in the geographic area comprising the European Union countries using the euro as a monetary unit are Eurobonds.

the stock being traded in two key ways. *First,* people noticed that the stock price was rising very rapidly. *Second,* people noticed that there was unusually high trading volume in the stock from fast, heavy buying by the manipulators.

When manipulators buy up a stock, they want to do everything possible to keep it a secret. This means that they don't want any obvious traces that they are doing it.

Few cases of manipulation hit the press. Manipulators do everything possible to stay hidden from the public. Because of this, the empirical literature in finance regarding this subject is very limited. The widespread manipulation through stock pool pump-and-dumps, the forerunners of today's mutual funds, before the crash of 1929 is vividly documented by Harvard economist **John Kenneth Galbraith.**[73] **Pump-and-dump schemes** today are usually in Nano-cap stocks. These schemes have also been detected in small markets like Pakistan.[74]

---

[73] Galbraith, A. J., 1972, *The Great Crash,* 1929, Boston: Houghton Mifflin Company.

[74] Khwaja, A., and A. Mian, 2004, "Unchecked Intermediaries: Price Manipulation in an Emerging Stock Market,: *Journal of Financial Economics,* forthcoming.

Chapter 9: International Investing

The U.S. banking systems' severe mismanagement of stock investor margin accounts resulted in laws that prohibit U.S. banks from acting as equity dealers. In Europe such prohibitions were never instated. European banks are known as "universal" banks, meaning you can walk into a bank and set up a checking, savings, and investing account all at the same time. This is a superior system if you are a savvy investor, but disaster otherwise—a banker cannot be a sophisticated advisor in these areas. In addition, this system makes it even easier for large financial interests behind the scenes to dump their stock holdings at high prices on uneducated investors. My friend Don was delighted to share his story in the hopes that he can help you from falling into the same trap as he—especially if you are a European stock investor reading this book. Don recounts:

"It was May of 2000, and a fine spring day in northern Spain. For the last three years I had worked for a Spanish construction company that built "American-style" hog farms. I had ascended rapidly through the company's ranks from production to construction site supervision, and finally into the engineering department. I was on a job

Trap: Both the 401(k) and the standard IRA blast you with huge fees for early withdrawal. For this reason, open a Roth IRA and Roth Solo K. You can withdraw your contributions tax-free in an emergency!

site near Pamplona—where tourists watch the running of the bulls—putting a farm into final operation when my supervisor told me that he wanted me in the home office in Barcelona by 1:00 Friday, the following day. It was a four-hour drive, which meant I would have to leave at 9:00 the next morning. I still had some work to finish up, but thought that I'd leave it for the following week. Besides, I had been out all week and I was looking forward to getting home for the weekend. The company had grown extremely fast over the last several years and was still going through some growing pains, so I didn't think much about the request to go to the home office. When I went into the "meeting" with my supervisor, he explained they were going through a downsizing and, since I was one of the higher paid employees, I had been selected to be laid off—right then and there—no two weeks' notice! He gave no reason other than that they made up their mind and said that they would pay the indemnification stipulated by law. That brought about a big change in my life, but it also gave us some unexpected money that we were able to use to our financial benefit. When I got paid, we took 25% of the money and decided that then was a good time to invest in the stock market. I didn't have any idea that insiders were dumping their holdings at the time on little guys like me coming into the markets with no experience. It was something that I had wanted to do for a long time, but with all the expenses of raising a family and my absence during most of the week, I had never had the time to look into stock investing or even set aside the money to do it. I checked with my bank, and they were promoting what seemed to be a good stock in Deutsche Telekom. I now strongly suspect that they were promoting the stock because they had large clients who had bought low years before who wanted out and, as Dr. Brown says, they were "making a market for the insiders." Deutsche Telecom was moving up, which made it look great to a novice like me, my banker explained how the mobile telephone market was booming and how the stock would continue to rise in price. On this strong recommendation from my banker, I bought as many shares as I could.

Making a long story short: about three years later, everything seemed to be in the dumpster. By 2003, the stock market tanked and I had begun my own business, which was eating up a lot of money to get it started and had required that I take out loans. As for the stocks, I had always heard that you never lost money with stocks in good companies, even if they had depreciated, unless you sell them—good companies always come back up in price. My new business made our finances tight, and we had to make our loan payments. The last thing I wanted to do was sell the stock, but we were running late on our business loan payments and the bank was pushing us to get caught up. I was forced by circumstance to sell all my shares of Deutsche Telecom at a loss.

This bitter experience made me think, "Forget about the stock market!" and I did. It wasn't until I was introduced to Dr. Brown, who patiently educated me about very basic yet vital things in the market that has given me confidence to even think about investing in it again. Scott is one of those people that you wish you would have met a long time ago. Scott and I met because my company is a publishing company that represents American authors in Europe, so I had the opportunity to pre-edit this book. As I read through the material, I was amazed at how he makes it easy for me to understand things about the market that every person should know before they make a decision to invest in stocks. When I told Scott my stock-investing story, the first thing he advised me was: "Don't ever trust your banker!" Well, I already knew that from experience, but what he continued to explain was that banks have way too many things to take care of on a daily basis to also be experts on investing in the stock market. They may be able to offer a particular stock or another, but the basics that you read about in this book they will never tell you."

Daniel Hall, J.D. of RealFastResults.com leads us in wishing you the greatest of family wealth through sound financial stewardship.

Thanks for choosing me as your financial mentor, — **Doc Brown**

Professor of Finance of the AACSB Accredited Graduate School of Business of the University of Puerto Rico

P.P.S. Discover how an 18-Year-Old McDonald's minimum wage cook becomes a millionaire in 50 years. Enroll in this essential community on stock investing now at http://worryfreewealth.com/offers/.

Index

points which can also adversely affect actual trading results. There are numerous other factors related to the markets. In general, or to the implementation of any specific trading program which cannot be fully accounted for in the preparation of hypothetical performance results and all of which can adversely affect actual trading results.

As costs vary among traders, including commission and fees, hypothetical trading examples usually do not always take commissions and fees into consideration. Please make sure you consider your individual cost of doing business in the form of commissions and fees.

CPSIA information can be obtained
at www.ICGtesting.com
Printed in the USA
FFOW03n0115030917
39487FF